MORE EQUALITY

HERBERT J. GANS

MORE
EQUALITY

VINTAGE BOOKS
A DIVISION OF RANDOM HOUSE
NEW YORK

FIRST VINTAGE BOOKS EDITION, November 1974
Copyright © 1968, 1969, 1972, 1973 by Herbert J. Gans

Portions of this book originally appeared
in the *American Journal of Sociology,*
the *New York Times,* and *Saturday Review.*

Library of Congress Cataloging in Publication Data
Gans, Herbert J.
More equality.
Bibliography: p.
    1. United States—Social conditions—1960–
2. Equality.   I. Title.
[HN65.G28   1974]   309.1′73′092   74–3339
ISBN 0–394–71167–X

FOR LOUISE AND DAVID

The more I advanced in the study of American society, the more I perceived that . . . equality of condition is the fundamental fact from which all others seem to be derived and the central point at which all my observations terminated. . . . The gradual development of the principle of equality is, therefore, a providential fact. It has all the chief characteristics of such a fact: it is universal, it is lasting, it constantly eludes all human interference, and all events as well as all men contribute to its progress. . . . [It is] an irresistible revolution which has advanced for centuries in spite of every obstacle.

Alexis de Tocqueville,
Democracy in America

CONTENTS

PREFACE

America can be described as an unequal society that would like to think of itself as egalitarian. While officially dedicated to equality of opportunity, to enabling the disadvantaged to succeed on the basis of their individual ambition and talent, America has not acted to remove the group handicaps—of class, race, and sex, among others—which prevent many people from actually realizing that opportunity. Rich and poor, for example, have an equal opportunity to work as common laborers, but the poor rarely obtain the education and social contacts that provide access to executive positions. Equality, therefore, cannot be defined solely in terms of opportunity; it must also be judged by *results*, by whether current inequalities of income and wealth, occupation, political power, and the like are being reduced.

This is a book of essays about equality of results, or rather, about *more* equality. It assumes that perfect or complete equality is not a realistic goal, albeit a proper topic for utopian thought. Instead, the book deals with the possibilities and problems of achieving greater equality, considering particularly the economic, social, political, and other consequences, including undesirable ones, that would follow in the wake of reducing inequality. As such, this is also a book about egalitarian policy, which attempts to look pragmatically at both the virtues and the vices of more equality and proposes specific policies for more equality of various kinds.

I think of equality, not as an end-state, but as the direction or trend of a social process that, as it leads to social change, creates costs as well as benefits. While the benefits of more equality may be obvious, at least to and for the present victims of inequality, the costs, both for the beneficiaries of inequality and for America as a whole, have to be identified and dealt with if egalitarian change is to come about.

A book about equality may appear otherworldly at a time when the Republican party has won a landslide election victory and is attempting, as it traditionally does, to redirect government policies in favor of its primary constituents, the beneficiaries of present inequalities. Nevertheless I believe, as I argue in the essays of Part I, that America is on the threshold of egalitarian change, and that in the years to come it will slowly begin to move toward more equality, partly because many Americans now favor policies that will make them more equal, but also because in the long run America cannot function and cohere as a society in any other way. For this reason, discussions and studies of what a more egalitarian America would look like, what problems it must solve, and what policy issues it must debate in becoming more egalitarian should be undertaken now.

This is one reason for my putting together the present collection of essays, some previously published, some new. There is another reason: very little is currently being written in favor of equality, at least in America, while at the same time, a number of able and influential social scientists are writing critical or at least skeptical articles about equality. Among the major social science critics are Edward Banfield, Milton Friedman, Arthur Jensen, Irving Kristol, and Robert Nisbet; the writers I would describe as skeptics include Daniel Bell, Nathan Glazer, Seymour M. Lipset, Daniel Patrick Moynihan, and James Wilson, among others. Although most of their work is published in academic journals, or quasi-academic ones like *Commentary* and *The Public Interest*, some also appears in the more popular media, thus creating a climate of published opinion that is becoming dangerously one-sided.

Much of what these writers say is not anti-egalitarian, and many of their observations concern problems egalitarian thinkers must come to grips with. Nevertheless, some of their writing is expressly anti-egalitarian—and it takes several forms.

First, the old notion that some people may be genetically incapable of more equality is being revived, even though the primary data are suspect IQ tests; even though there is mounting evidence that intelligence, particularly as measured by such tests, has little to do with occupational and social performance; and even though intelligence cannot be the sole criterion for treating people as equals.

A second argument is that too much concern with equality is irrelevant, since it is already on the way. For example, the December 1972 issue of *Fortune* carried an article showing that economic inequality is declining, even though the government's *Monthly Labor Review* came out that same month with an article by Peter Henle, citing his own and other researchers' data that showed it was in fact increasing. Another version of this argument claims that inequality has decreased over the last hundred years, and even though this is true, those Americans unhappy about today's inequality and with high expectations for economic improvement are not likely to be much interested in historical comparisons. Defenders of the now defunct Family Assistance Plan have celebrated it as a dramatic income-redistribution scheme, even though it would have raised incomes for only some welfare recipients in about eight states and for the poorest of the working poor. Another version of this argument suggests that the dangers of inequality have been overrated, and that whereas wealth could once buy power and deference, this is no longer true, even though the presidents of the big corporations are still buying both except perhaps on the campus.

A third argument has it that however desirable equality is in principle, it is unworkable in practice. One approach here is to show the impracticality of complete equality, even though this is a straw man of limited relevance to the topic of more equality. Another approach I call capitalist-realist: it demonstrates that policies for more equality would have disastrous effects particularly on the people most victimized by inequality, even though such demonstrations almost always assume that nineteenth-century capitalist procedures are still being practiced in this society and cannot be abrogated (except that the federal government abrogates them constantly for the politically powerful). A more persuasive form of this argument warns that the ability of government to bring about change by egalitarian social policy is limited, even though the limits are often illustrated by past government policies so underfinanced or faulty in conception that experts, at least, knew from the start that they would fail. A variation on this theme generalizes from the admitted limits of some policies to argue that there are fixed limits to all policies, even though, for example, the inability of higher welfare benefits to alter family patterns dramatically does not mean that such benefits may not improve the economic lot of welfare recipients.

A fourth argument claims that Americans are not really interested in equality, but want some other good which can be achieved without drastic tampering with the status quo. They are said to want less bureaucracy, but even though this may be accurate, they also want a kind of debureaucratization that increases their power vis-à-vis the government, and thus more political equality. A different approach is to equate egalitarianism with populism and then to sneer at it because of the ideological and other shortcomings of the earlier Populists, even though the two "movements" are quite different and the argument just tars the current demands for more equality with a historical brush. The most extreme formulation of the fourth argument claims that the concern with equality is just another plot by intellectuals to stir up the relatively contented American populace, even though almost all of the egalitarian demands I describe in Part I were not initiated by intellectuals. Besides, intellectuals are also people, and occasionally they express ideas that are either being felt more inchoately by nonintellectuals, or are about to be so felt.

The final argument is to question the motives of the proponents of more equality, even though motives have nothing to do with the validity of propositions. The proponents of more equality are, it is charged, not really interested in equality, but (1) are guilt-ridden over their own affluence; or (2) are looking for a messianic cause to replace religion and to fill their own spiritually empty lives; or (3) are out to create a more altruistic society, using equality as a new weapon against the bourgeois ethos they have allegedly always opposed; or (4) want to gain power for themselves; or (5) are radicals who despite some new language are just demonstrating old-time Stalinist inclinations.

This book will not rebut the various anti-egalitarian arguments, except parenthetically, but I must note that in writing these essays, I have either read or met personally almost all of the contemporary proponents of more equality, and I have yet to find anyone harboring such motives. Whether they are long-time socialists, or newly radicalized, or apolitical—as some are—they are concerned about the economic and other injustices of this society or find equality a relevant intellectual topic. Undoubtedly they have other, more personal motives, but these have not surfaced in their writings or in our conversations. In any case, I can speak only for myself about motives, but want to say that I am contentedly agnostic and am not looking for a secular messianic movement; do not want to establish an altruistic society (and believe that any egalitarian policies based on expectations of altruism are doomed to fail); have no quarrel with the bourgeois ethos; am not seeking any power other than that of persuasion (which I think is proper for writers); and am not a radical. I admit to feeling some guilt about the existing inequalities of America, and even more about that of the rest of the world in comparison with America, but I also have misgivings about the likelihood that in a more egalitarian society my income will be reduced and some of my privileges will disappear. I do not look forward to either, but would accept both as the price of a more egalitarian society, and expect to derive some vicarious satisfaction from the benefits going to those now less fortunate than I.

Undoubtedly the skeptics and critics of equality also have their motives, but I shall not guess at or impugn them. Some of them are friends of long standing, and I find it unpleasant just to have to disagree with them. I should repeat that their arguments are by no means all specious or wrong, or as some have suggested, mere rationalizations of their own high economic, social, and cultural position. What I find distressing—on the part of many but not all of the above-mentioned—is the mood of their writing; their overriding attention to the costs of equality without recognition of the benefits; their positive assessment of the status quo, which sometimes reflects their lack of contact with people less fortunate than they and sometimes their feeling that such people do not really matter; their apparent glee in demonstrating that egalitarian change must make things worse; their narrow-minded defense of the contemporary academic meritocracy, as if its present incumbents had all been chosen on merit alone and were all as meritorious and prolific as they are; and above all, their frequently impatient and sometimes irritable tone in discussing both the arguments for and the proponents of more equality.

Finally, a note about what this book does not cover. To begin with, it pays only passing attention to the analysis of existing inequalities, for they are currently being well documented by a number of social scientists and journalists. Also, it does not make a moral case for more equality. This case has been made in recent times by, among others, R. H. Tawney and Richard M. Titmuss, two powerful thinkers to whom I, like all contemporary writers about equality, am immensely indebted. Besides, one has only to visit the slums and low-income neighborhoods of this allegedly affluent country to come away with sufficient moral grounds for more equality. Nor do I go into the philosophical bases and issues of equality, except as they pertain to egalitarian policy, and the book does not even mention Babeuf, Mill, Rousseau, and, aside from John Rawls, more recent philosophers of equality. Finally, the book does not pretend to be a systematic treatment of more equality; it is, rather, a collection of ideas and observations upon the topic. Even so, I hope it will contribute to the egalitarian position in the current debate, and will encourage others to delve more thoroughly into the subject.

THE ORGANIZATION OF THE BOOK

The book consists of three parts. In Part I, I describe the changes in American life and American attitudes that convince me the country is moving toward more equality, and the latter half of Chapter One summarizes my own ideas about how this ought to happen and what egalitarian policies are most desirable or necessary. In Part II, I begin by defining what I mean by equality, go on to discuss some of the problems of egalitarian policy and some of the economic, social, and political obstacles to more equality, ending this part of the book with a chapter on the likelihood of—and policies for—income redistribution, which I think will be on the political agenda in the not-so-distant future and may be the first instance of more equality actually to be achieved. This chapter is also the concluding essay for the policy-oriented portion of the book, for Part III is written mainly for researchers and utopians. Chapter Seven proposes a number of immediately useful equality researches, while Chapter Eight presents several "utopian scenarios" describing hypothetical societies with various kinds of complete equality—economic, political, sexual, and familial among others. Despite my doubts about the

relevance of complete equality, the utopian exercise under-
lines more starkly the sorts of issues that will come up in
policy aimed at more equality. An epilogue brings the book
down to earth again, assessing the prospects of more
equality in the light of current political happenings that
threaten to plunge America into greater inequality.

ACKNOWLEDGMENTS

Most of the people to whom I am indebted are named in
the footnotes and bibliography, but a number with whom
I have exchanged ideas that appear in this book deserve
specific mention: Susan Ferge, Peter Marris, S. M. Miller,
Frances Piven, Martin Rein, and especially Lee Rainwater.
Some of the ideas in Chapters Three and Eight came out
of a seminar on equality which I taught with Rainwater
when I was on the MIT faculty. I am particularly grateful
to Frances Piven for reading the manuscript on short
notice, and for her many helpful comments. Others
helped me by critically reading one or more chapters:
Peter Marris (Chapters Three and Four), Robert K. Merton (Chapter Four), S. M. Miller (Chapters Four and Six),
Joseph Pechman (Chapter Six), Lee Rainwater (Chapters
Three and Six), and Alvin Schorr (Chapter Six). I am also
grateful to Columbia University for giving me time to do
research and writing; to the Center for Policy Research for
secretarial and other aid; and to the *New York Times
Magazine, Saturday Review,* and the *American Journal of
Sociology* for permission to reprint articles that appeared
there first. Alice Liftin typed the manuscript quickly and
impeccably, and Jeanne Morton of Pantheon Books helped
with superb copy-editing. I owe a special debt to my wife,
Louise, for in sharing with me her experience as an anti-

poverty lawyer in the slums of New York and Boston, she provided me with at least some indirect contact with the major victims of inequality from whom a university professor is too often isolated. She also read the manuscript and made many useful suggestions. The faults of the book are my own.

H.G.

March 1973

I
EGALITARIAN TRENDS IN AMERICA

INTRODUCTION

As the preface suggests, I believe America is heading for more equality of results, by which I mean a greater similarity in income and political influence among income, occupational, racial, ethnic, and age groups and the sexes. (A more detailed definition of equality can be found on pp. 63–73.) The first essays in the book discuss this egalitarian trend, making two somewhat different but related arguments. Chapter One points to the demands for political change which began to be voiced during the 1960s by blacks, students, women, public service employees, blue-collar workers, and many others, and which continue to be voiced in the 1970s, albeit in less visible and militant forms. These demands do not always call for more equality, however, and often ask for more liberty, but they are egalitarian in their consequences, for they require some reduction of power, control, and even income on the part of the targets of these demands. For example, while many blue-collar workers are currently asking, not for equality, but for an improvement in working conditions

3

and some control over the assembly-line process, the outcome of their demands will inevitably reduce the power of management and thus make labor-management relations somewhat more equal.

The making of demands is not, however, equivalent to achieving them. Not only are the beneficiaries of existing inequalities politically powerful, but the demanders are by no means a united force, although both Senators Robert Kennedy and George McGovern attempted to make them into a coalition. In fact, the demands of one group sometimes contradict those of another, and some groups are opposed to the demands of others. For example, while white blue-collar workers are demanding more control over their lives, they are frequently opposed to blacks making much the same demand. Consequently, whose demands will be met, and to what extent, remains uncertain, although I also suggest that both the American economy and the American polity have always bent to demands when sufficient political pressure was exerted.

Chapter Two, though originally written about the mood of malaise and despair that began to grip America in the late 1960s, makes somewhat the same argument from another set of observations. It notes the rising expectations for a higher standard of living, particularly in Middle America, which developed as a result of the affluence that followed World War II, the increased demand for government intervention in the economy to protect that standard in bad economic times, and a call now just beginning for more responsible performances by both government and the economy, which is reflected in the growth of the ecology and consumer movements, among others.

These changes in the public mood are not merely changes in attitudes, but responses to changing conditions in American society. The opportunity to become economically independent, either as an entrepreneur, a small businessman, or an independent professional, has evaporated sufficiently for most Americans to realize that they will always be employees and that they can best promote their own interests by demanding change from employers, and from government as it increasingly participates in the economy. Moreover, the decline of economic growth, the acceptance—at least among the middle class—of the need for ecological restrictions to growth, and the fear of the effects of automation on the availability of work, especially among blue-collar and semiskilled office workers, are forcing people to realize that economic growth alone is no longer the guarantor of increasing affluence, at least for them, that it used to be. These changes in the economy may therefore spur people to realize that they can achieve affluence instead through a greater sharing of the available wealth and income.

Similarly, the increasing centralization of both the economy and the government is making ordinary citizens more powerless at the same time that their rising educational and political sophistication is making them feel they need more power to control their own lives, which may produce demands for more political equality.

But even if the political pressures for more economic and political equality do not materialize, I argue that a society as large and diverse as America cannot long continue to function effectively or cohere without more equality, that it can deal constructively with its political conflicts only if differences in self-interest that stem from sharp inequalities of income and power can be ameliorated, and that therefore it needs to be more egalitarian. Societies do not always do what they need to do, of course, but the malaise I describe in Chapter Two will not end until that need is met.

If more equality of results is and ought to be coming, a variety of crucial policy issues must be considered and debated, such as what kinds of equality are most important, how much equality is necessary and desirable, and perhaps above all, how equality can be reconciled with the powerful tradition of American individualism. These issues are discussed in more detail in Part II, but they are also taken up in the last half of Chapter One, which is therefore a brief overview of the remainder of the book.

1
The Equality Revolution

Someday, when future historians write the history of the 1960s, they may describe it as the decade when America rediscovered the poverty still in its midst and when social protest, ranging from demonstrations to violent uprisings, reappeared on the American scene. But these historians may also note a curious fact, that the social protest had very little to do with poverty. Most of the demonstrators and marchers who followed Martin Luther King were not poor; the college students who protested and sat-in on campus were well-to-do, and even the participants in the ghetto uprisings, although hardly affluent, were not drawn from the poorest sectors of the ghetto.

The social protest that began in the 1960s has to do with *inequality*. So far the demand for greater equality has come largely from the young, from the black, and from women, but other groups have asked for more autonomy or control over their own lives, for more liberty and democracy, demands that also have egalitarian implications even though they are not directly egalitarian in motive. In the years to come, I believe America will face more such demands from many other people, which will be widespread enough that they might be described as an "equality revolution," at least in the popular American if not the classic European and Marxist sense. The demand for more equality will bring about many changes in American life, but the revolution of which I write is unlikely to be violent.

THE NATURE OF THE EQUALITY REVOLUTION

In a large and complex society, inequality and the lack of control over one's life are pervasive, and are often thought to be inevitable by-products of modernity and affluence. The protest that began in the sixties suggests, however, that they are not inevitable, and that there can be more democracy, autonomy—and equality—but only if enough people want them and are willing to act politically to achieve their demands.

Historically, these demands can perhaps be traced back to the day in 1955 when Mrs. Rosa Parks of Montgomery, Alabama, decided that she was no longer willing to sit in the rear of the bus, and to the time when black Southern college students demonstrated against the legal and political inequality with which they were saddled. Since then, other blacks have argued for racial equality through Black Power. Although only a decade or so ago they seemed to want integration, the right to become part of the white community, they have now recognized that white America offers integration to only a token few and requires assimilation into the white majority as the price of integration. Consequently, many young blacks are asking to be separate but equal. When they say that black is beautiful, they are really saying that black is equal to white, and when the ghetto demands control of its own institutions, it is asking for the right to have the same control over its community that many white communities have long enjoyed.

A second major source of equality demands has been among college students, and more recently, high school students. Whatever the immediate causes of the various campus protests and uprisings, the students who have participated in them seem to agree on two demands: to be treated as adults and to participate in the governing of their schools. Headline-making demonstrations have fallen off in recent years, but these student demands have not disappeared, even among those who have now returned to more private goals, and they will be revived when more effective strategies for achieving them turn up.

Women's liberation is also a demand for more equality, and in the few years that the movement has existed, it has spread beyond the upper-middle-class circles where it began. Many women in the lower middle class, while not about to participate in liberation politics, are beginning to ask themselves similar questions, and are perhaps asking them of their husbands also. In fact, the equality revolution has probably proceeded further in the home than anywhere else; in the last two generations, women, at least in the middle class, have achieved more equality in the home than any other group anywhere else. They now often divide the housework with their husbands, and in recent years, they have extended the quest for equality to the right to enjoy sex on an equal basis with men.

Similarly, adolescents have appealed for the same

sexual freedom now available to young adults, and more quietly, they have been obtaining the right to freedom of choice in their leisure-time activities. Even preteens are now asking for their own "youth culture."

Man's relationship to God and the church is also moving toward greater equality. The minister is no longer a theological father; in many synagogues and Protestant churches he has become the servant of his congregation, and the unwillingness of many Catholics to abide by the pope's dictates on birth control and other matters indicates their rejection of dogma that is handed down from on high. The real meaning of the God Is Dead Movement, I believe, is that the old conception of God as infallible autocrat has been rejected.

Similar egalitarian developments have been occurring in the economy and the polity. Wage workers have begun to demand the same guaranteed annual incomes and other privileges that salaried workers have; public employees have struck for wage equity with workers in private industry; assembly-line workers have sought better working conditions, more control over the operation of the line, and thus more autonomy in their work; and enlisted men have called for reductions in the power of officers. Skilled service workers have attempted to transform their occupations into professions so that they can obtain more autonomy in their work; and employed professionals such as teachers, social workers, journalists, and athletes have resorted to strikes for the same purpose. Even welfare recipients have argued and demonstrated for the right to be treated with more respect—not to mention fairness—although they have perhaps been less successful in achieving their demands than anyone else.

The growing consumer movement also has egalitarian implications, for insofar as consumers are calling for more influence over what goods are to be produced and sold, they are attempting to reduce the unequal relationship between themselves and the manufacturers. And in the few cases where stockholders are demanding a greater role in the decisions of management, they are also demanding a change in what is currently a highly unequal and undemocratic relationship.

At the national level, politics is being transformed by two thrusts. On the one hand, politically active citizens have rejected the traditional autocracy and "boss rule" of the political party organization, at least among the Democrats, and the increasing number of voters who cast a split ticket suggests that they, too, are ready to become more independent. But perhaps the greatest change has taken place among working-class people. In responding favorably to men like Governor Wallace and Vice-President Agnew, they are in effect saying that they are tired of being represented by upper-class politicians and of being ruled by the upper-middle-class experts whom Governor Wallace calls "pseudo-intellectuals"; they want a president who will bring working-class concerns into the making of public policy and will treat working-class people as a more equal part of his constituency. The recent revival of ethnic identity among the descendants of European immigrants of the late nineteenth century is another instance of this demand; many of the newly self-conscious ethnic groups are not interested in reviving their traditional cultures but in obtaining more political influence, and the demands they make are rarely ethnic in substance. Rather, they closely resemble the demands made by nonethnic working-class people; not surprisingly, considering that many "ethnics" are still employed in blue-collar or unskilled white-collar jobs.

At the local level, the search for more equality began

soon after World War II. Although the exodus to suburbia took place primarily because people sought better homes and neighborhoods, they also wanted to obtain greater control over governmental institutions than is available in the city. In the last twenty years, the new suburbanites have overthrown many of the rural political machines that used to run the suburbs, establishing governments that respond to their demands for low taxes and the exclusion of poorer and darker newcomers. Their efforts have been followed by the call for community control among some urban residents, and with it the attempt to obtain more power over their neighborhoods. Since then, community control has broadened into a larger movement to reduce the power of bureaucracies at all levels of government and of professionals over their clients: for example, of doctors over patients, teachers over parents, and planners over homeowners.

As I noted earlier, it must be emphasized that these various demands are more often concerned with autonomy and democracy than with equality per se. In addition, they are not made by a single movement, and are sometimes even contradictory or in opposition; they are actually a concurrent series of independent and sometimes diametrically different stirrings on the part of quite diverse populations. Blacks and women are both seeking more equality, but they are not united and not likely to unite, for they are driven apart by many differences. Many black men, struggling to reduce the superior economic and social status of women in the black community, do not look kindly on women's liberation, and even less so on a group that is still predominantly upper middle class and almost entirely white. White union members come together with their black colleagues to demand better working conditions, but oppose the latter when they seek better housing in white neighborhoods. Journalists struggle against the unilateral

power of editors, but, as sports fans, may resent the professional athletes who strike to reduce the power of team
owners.

In addition, the demanding groups vary in size and
make-up; many are small, and they differ in age, class, education, race, and other characteristics. Some are politically
militant and want to change society as a whole; others are
conservative, hoping to reclaim the past—for instance, the
whites who want to put blacks back into an earlier place
and the adults who want to do likewise with adolescents.

An aggregate of dissatisfied groups with conflicting
demands can hardly be described as constituting a trend,
much less an equality revolution, at least in terms of their
intent, but I think they constitute both in terms of *outcome. If all these demands are looked at together, they
mean more income for some and higher costs for others;
more rights for some and fewer privileges for others; more
power for some and less control for others. And if the demands grow into significant political pressures that have to
be satisfied, the eventual outcome will have to be greater
equality, although not necessarily for all those demanding
change, nor of a kind that necessarily coincides with their
demands.*

INEQUALITY IN AMERICA

Whatever the final outcome, the demands I have described
are too widespread to be explained away as the plaints of
discontented minorities; they are, among other things, re-
flections of the many kinds of inequality that now exist in
America. The most important inequality is probably economic; though America may be an affluent society for some
people, income and wealth are distributed quite unequally.
The poorest fifth of all Americans obtain only about 3

percent of the country's annual income and own less than half of 1 percent of its wealth. The next poorest fifth get 11 percent of the income and hold an estimated 2 percent of the wealth. Conversely, the richest fifth receive 46 percent of the annual income and own 77 percent of the wealth, and the very richest one-twentieth of the population, 20 percent of the income and 53 percent of the wealth. And 7 percent of all income but fully one-third of all the wealth belongs to 1 percent of the people.[1] While many Americans now own some stocks, 2 percent of all individual stockholders own about two-thirds of the individually held stocks.[2]

The same inequality exists in the business world. Of the almost 2 million corporations in America, one-tenth of 1 percent control 55 percent of total corporate assets; and 1.1 percent, 82 percent. At the other end of the spectrum, 94 percent of the corporations own only 9 percent of the total assets.[3] Even the public economy is unequal, for the poor pay a larger share of their income for taxes than anyone else; people earning less than $2,000 pay fully half their income in taxes as compared to only 45 percent paid by those earning $50,000 or more. Moderate-income groups are not much better off; people getting $8,000 to $10,000 a year pay only 4 percent less of their income than those making $25,000 to $50,000.[4] As these figures suggest, many American taxes are regressive, particularly state and local sales and property taxes—and social security. But even the federal income tax is not very progressive; in 1966, for example, the income share of the poorest 40 percent of the population was exactly the same after federal income taxes had been paid as before, while that of the richest fifth declined by only 2 percent after tax payments and that of the next richest fifth increased by the same amount.[5]

Of course, the poor get something back from the government through welfare and other transfer payments,[6] but then so do the affluent, especially through indirect subsidies in the guise of tax policies, such as the capital-gains tax preference and the tax exemptions granted to municipal-bond purchasers. Philip Stern, author of *The Rape of the Taxpayer* and himself a multimillionaire, described these subsidies as "a welfare program that reverses the usual pattern and gives huge welfare payments to the super-rich but only pennies to the very poor," and estimated that the annual subsidies came to $720,000 per family for people with million-dollar incomes, $650 per family for the $10,000–$15,000 middle-income group, and $16 per family for the poor earning under $3,000. This welfare program, he went on to say, "goes by the name of the Internal Revenue Code of 1954 as amended. It is the basic income tax law of the United States."[7]

Similarly, some years ago Alvin Schorr analyzed all federal housing programs and determined that the government spent three and a half times as much in subsidies for middle- and upper-income housing as for public housing for the poor.[8] A recent study of educational subsidies in California showed that the state's universities, which serve the more affluent students, received an average annual subsidy per student of $4,870, while the junior colleges, which serve the less affluent students, received only $1,050.[9]

But there are other kinds of economic inequality in America as well. For example, most good jobs today require at least a bachelor's degree, but many moderate-income families still cannot afford to send their children to college. Job security is also distributed unequally. College professors have tenure and are assured of a lifetime job; professionals and white-collar workers earn a salary and are rarely laid off even in depressions; factory workers, service workers, and migrant farm laborers are still paid by the hour and those not unionized can be laid off at a moment's notice.

Economic inequality extends beyond income and job security. Some executives and white-collar workers have a say in how their work is to be done, but most other workers can still be fired for talking back to the boss (and are then ineligible for unemployment compensation). Generally speaking, most work places, whether they are offices or factories, are run on an autocratic basis; employees are inherently unequal and have no more right to determine their work, their working conditions, or the governance of their places of work than enlisted men in the armed services. They are only cogs in a large machine, and have about as much influence over their work as cogs. Many schools are similarly autocratic; neither in college nor in elementary and high school do students have any significant rights in the classroom; they are unequal citizens who must obey the teacher if they are to graduate.

The poor suffer most from these inequalities. They hold the most insecure jobs, they are least often union members, and if they are on welfare, they can be made penniless if they displease the social worker in charge of their case. And being poor, they pay more for everything.[10] They even pay more when they gamble. Affluent Americans can gamble in the stock market, but the poor can only afford to play the numbers, where the chance of a "hit" is about 600 to 1, and if they prefer not to participate in an illegal activity, they can play a state lottery, and in New York the chance of winning is only about 4,000 to 1.

Political inequality is also rampant. For example, since about 12 percent of the population are poor in terms of the official poverty line, an egalitarian political system would require that about 50 congressmen and 12 senators represent or speak for the poor. This is not the case, however, even though big business, big labor, and even less numerous sectors of the population have their unofficial representatives in both houses of Congress. While Supreme Court action has finally brought about the "one person, one vote" principle in electing these representatives, the seniority system maintains the traditional pattern of inequality, so that a handful of congressmen and senators, many from rural districts, still hold much of the real power on Capitol Hill. Affluent individuals and well-organized interest groups actually have more than one vote per person because they have far greater access to their elected representatives than the ordinary citizen, and because they can afford to hire lobbyists who watch out for their interests and even help to write legislation.

In most states, tenants, children, and adolescents have almost no legal rights to speak of, and many moderate-income families have unequal access to legal and medical services because they are not poor enough to qualify for public programs and are too poor to afford private ones. There is even a considerable degree of cultural inequality, for the museums and cultural centers that cater most to the affluent population are subsidized by public funds, while moderate-income people must pay for much of their culture and entertainment, at least indirectly, since they obtain these largely from the commercial media; and the poor, who have so little purchasing power that the mass media are not interested in them, are virtually deprived of culture and entertainment that speak to their needs. Finally, there are other inequalities which have not even been so described as yet, although they touch almost every person. For example, the individuals who are included in the sample of the now-so-important opinion polls cannot tell the pollster that his questions may be loaded or badly worded.

These patterns of inequality are not new, and although America has sometimes been described as a nation of equals and a classless society, this is a myth. To be sure, America never had the well-defined classes or estates that existed in Europe, but from its beginning it has nevertheless been a nation of unequals. For example, in 1774, among the minority of Philadelphians affluent enough to pay taxes, 10 percent owned fully 89 percent of the taxable property.[11] A study of wealth in Baltimore, New Orleans, and St. Louis in the 1860s showed that the poorest fifth owned none of the wealth; the richest fifth owned 93 percent; the richest one-twentieth, 73 percent; and the top 1 percent, 45 percent—although in rural areas, wealth was distributed a little more equally.[12] Over the last hundred years, the degree of economic inequality has been reduced somewhat, but in the last sixty years, since relatively reliable statistics on income distribution have been available, that distribution has changed little.[13] Moreover, several recent studies have shown that income inequality has been rising again during the last ten years.[14]

It may be unfair to call the idea of the nation of equals just a myth, for it has also been a persisting ideal in American life from the beginning—except that it has never been pursued very energetically in either the economy or the polity. Even the ideal that every boy could be president of the United States or of General Motors has rarely been achieved; most of our presidents have been rich, and studies of the origins of American businessmen show that in the nineteenth century as now, the large majority were themselves sons of businessmen.

Impatience with Inequality

Nevertheless, over the last two hundred years most Americans seem to have put up quietly with the prevailing inequality, although historians rarely record the discontent of the most unequal, since these leave few documents for historical study. Today, however, the traditional patience with inequality has disappeared, and for three reasons.

First, many Americans are now beginning to realize that the frontier, by which I mean the opportunity to strike out on one's own and perhaps to strike it rich, is closing down. The literal frontier in the West was closed before the turn of the century, but until recently, other frontiers were still thought to be open. Rural people hoped that they could become independent by saving up for a farm; factory workers, by going into business, perhaps opening a gas station or a small workshop; and middle-class people, by entering the independent professions.

Today, these hopes have begun to evaporate, for the family farm is economically obsolete, the small store cannot compete with the chain, and the independent professions now consist more and more of salaried employees. Of course, there are still exceptions, and every year a few well-publicized individuals strike it rich, but their small number only proves the rule. Some Americans are now starting to realize that they will spend their working lives as employees, and that as employees they can best improve their fortunes by making demands on their employers and, because the government's role in the economy is rapidly increasing, on their political representatives.

Second, many people have become aware that as the bureaucracies and corporations grow bigger and American society becomes more centralized, the average individual becomes more powerless. Indeed, many of the demands for change that sprang up during the 1960s were fledgling attempts to overcome powerlessness and to redress the political imbalance.

Third, as I argue in Chapter Two, the affluence of the era following World War II has enabled many Americans to raise their incomes sufficiently so that they are no longer preoccupied solely with making ends meet. As a result, new expectations have emerged, not only for a higher standard of living but also for improvements in the quality of life and for greater power to control one's destiny. And more than ever before, people believe that the economy and the government should help them achieve their new expectations.

THE EFFECTS OF INEQUALITY

Once upon a time, inequality helped to make America great, for the country was built with the energy of restless entrepreneurs, the labor supplied by the unequal, and the capital generated from both. Today, inequality is a major source of social instability and unrest and even a cause of the rising rates of crime, delinquency, and social pathology —alcoholism, drug addiction, and mental illness, for example. The conventional wisdom has it that crime and pathology are largely caused by poverty, but during the 1960s, poverty declined sharply even while crime and pathology increased.[15] In these same years, however, inequality did not decrease, and depending on the figures used, actually grew worse. One conventional measure of inequality is the number of people who earn less than half the median family income. Between 1960 and 1970, when the median (as reported by the United States census) rose from $5,620 to $9,870, the number earning half that amount dropped only 1 percent, from 20 to 19. One can also define inequality by measuring the distance between the poverty line and the median income. In 1960, the poverty line came to 50 percent of the median; by 1970, it came to only 40 percent.[16] In other words, during the decade the poverty line rose far more slowly than the median income, and the inequality gap between the poor and the median earner actually widened.

This gap is not just economic, however; it also has social and emotional consequences. Being unequal results in feelings of inferiority, and these in turn generate inadequacy and self-hate or anger. Feelings of inadequacy and self-hate more than poverty help to account for the high rates of pathology; while anger results in crime, delinquency, senseless violence—and of course in political protest as well. But inequality also has less dramatic consequences. For example, some poor mothers refuse to send their children to school because they cannot afford to dress them properly; shabby clothes may protect a youngster from the elements—a flour sack made into a suit or dress would do that—but shabby clothes also mark the child as unequal, and mothers want to protect their children from this feeling even at the cost of depriving them of schooling. And if a father cannot find work, not only will his child's feelings of inferiority be more intense, but the child may justifiably conclude that it is doomed to the same fate, and that there is no reason for staying in school or continuing to hope for a fair shake from "the system."

The social and emotional consequences of inequality are also felt by moderate-income people, especially the almost 40 percent of Americans who earn above the poverty line but below the median income. For example, many young factory workers now realize—as their fathers could not afford to realize—that they hold unpleasant jobs without much chance of advancement or escape, and that much blue-collar work is inferior to the white-collar jobs that are now the norm in the American economy.[17] In fact, the pathology and protest normally associated with the poor are beginning to develop among factory workers as well. Hard drugs are now showing up in blue-collar neighborhoods, and strikes over working conditions—such as the one at the General Motors plant in Lordstown, Ohio, which made the headlines in 1972—are increasing in number and intensity.

Indeed, if the most serious inequalities in American life are not corrected, the people who feel themselves most unequal are likely to find new ways of getting even with America. New kinds of ghetto unrest, school, factory, and office disturbances, and dropping out of the system can be expected, and more crime in middle-class urban neighborhoods and suburbs is likely, for crime has always been a way by which at least some poor people obtained a primitive kind of income redistribution when society paid no heed to their inequality.

Inequality does not harm just the unequal; it hurts the entire society. The last ten years have demonstrated the fragility of the American political fabric, but the social fabric is also weak. Old sources of social stability have disappeared, and so has much of the traditional American culture that once provided satisfactions even under inegalitarian conditions. The small towns and rural areas which gave some people a sense of rootedness that made up for lack of affluence are being depleted by outmigration. In the cities, the ethnic cultures that maintained the peasants' necessary resignation to European inequality and provided group cohesion and a close-knit family life as compensation have now been Americanized. Although a revival of ethnic identity may be taking place currently, the old cultures are not being resuscitated, for as I noted earlier, the new ethnic identity is political and actually calls for more equality for ethnic groups.

In fact, Americans today are increasingly "members" of a single mainstream culture, divided into subcultures by differences in income, education, and the opportunity to obtain the goods and services which go with that culture. The subcultures themselves are by no means alike, but they share some important mainstream values, sometimes labeled the American Way of Life: individual and familial comfort, security and self-improvement, and the desirability of striving for ever higher levels of these, supported by ever-rising expectations that these levels will be achieved. These values differ sharply from those of traditional rural and ethnic cultures, which call for modest expectations for comfort, security, and self-improvement and therefore imply acceptance of or resignation to the prevailing inequality.

The continued rise in expectations makes it likely that America will enter a period of greater economic and political conflict, for when almost everyone has higher expectations, there must inevitably be conflict over how these expectations are to be met and whose are to be met first and foremost. America has always endured conflict, of course—after all, economic competition is itself a form of conflict—but conflict can tear society apart unless it is resolved constructively. This, however, is possible only if the participants in the conflict have, and feel they have, a chance to get what they want, and when this is not feasible, to get about as much as everyone else; in other words, if the conflict ends in a compromise that meets everyone's needs as fairly as possible. But if the participants in the conflict are unequal, those with power and wealth will almost always get what they want, whether from government or from the economy.

Conflicts can best be compromised fairly if the society is more egalitarian, if differences of self-interest that result from sharp inequality of income and power can be reduced. The more egalitarian a society, the greater the similarity of interests among its citizens, and the greater the likelihood that disagreements among them can be settled through fair compromise. Only in a more egalitarian society is it possible to develop policies that are truly in the public interest, for only in such a society do enough citizens share enough interests so that these can be considered public ones.[18]

A More Egalitarian Society

Consequently, the time has come to start thinking about a more egalitarian America, and to develop a model of equality that combines the traditional emphasis on the pursuit of liberty with the newly emerging need to reduce inequality. As Daniel Patrick Moynihan put it in the famous "Moynihan Report" of 1965, Equality of Opportunity must be transformed into Equality of Results. Equality of Opportunity simply enables people with more income and better education to win out over the less fortunate even when the competition itself is equitable, but Equality of Results means that people begin the competition more equal in these resources so that the outcome is also more egalitarian. Equality of Results does not mean absolute equality, either of income or any other resource, but sufficient reductions in present inequalities to erase handicaps in the competition.

Methods or models for achieving equality have historically been *collectivist*; they have called for increasing equality by replacing private institutions with public agencies to take over the allocation of resources, typically by nationalizing industry. This approach assumes that all resources belong equally to all people, and that public ownership will bring about equality. When all the people own everything, however, they really do not own anything, enabling the officials who govern in the name of the people to make themselves more-than-equal and to restrict political liberties. This seems to be an almost inevitable outcome of collectivist policies, at least in poor countries, even though these policies have also reduced over-all economic inequality.

An American equality model must be *individualistic*; it must achieve sufficient equality to allow the pursuit of liberty to continue but without restricting equal access to liberty for others. An individualistic model of equality begins with these assumptions: that people are not ready to stop competing for material or nonmaterial gain—and self-improvement—for the sake of equality; that they will not become altruists who repress their ego needs for the public good; and that they are not ready to surrender control over their lives to a government, however democratic, which doles out liberty and equality through collective ownership of all resources. Consequently, an individualistic model would aim for greater economic equality, not by nationalizing industry, but—among other things—by distributing stock ownership to larger numbers of people.[19] Similarly, individualistic equality would not mean providing the same public or private services to everyone; rather, it would attempt to equalize income and then let people spend that income on goods and services of their own choosing. While the extension of public services, particularly free ones, is an important method for bringing about more equality and is essential in some cases—for example, in medical services—I would argue that free choice should be maximized whenever possible, and for this goal, an income strategy is preferable to a services strategy. For instance, while it might be more efficient to equalize access to transportation by building mass-transit systems, I think it would be more desirable, except in high-

density cities, to give everyone enough income to buy a car
—and even to give free cars to the poor—because the freedom of movement and choice inherent in the car is more
in tune with America's individualistic tradition than mass
transit. (Maximum freedom of individual choice would of
course be obtained if people had access to both cars and
mass transit, but in low-density America this would be
too costly.) Finally, the individualistic model would not
call for every person getting the same income; rather, it
would enable people to maximize their earnings through
their own efforts, and would then create more equality
through tax and subsidy policies, as in Sweden and England.

EQUALITY AND LIBERTY

These observations suggest that the future will bring many
kinds of change to America, with new ideas coming to the
fore that question beliefs and values thought to be sacro-
sanct. The demands for change will of course be fought
bitterly, protests by backlash, and new ideas by old ones.
Today, some argue that college students are still children
and should not be given a voice in college administration,
just as some claim that women belong in the home. Undoubtedly, the defenders of outmoded traditions will argue
sincerely, with some facts and logic on their side, but processes of social change have little to do with sincerity, facts,
or logic. When people become dissatisfied with what they
have and demand something better, they cannot be de-
terred by facts or logic, and even the repression of new ideas
and new modes of behavior is effective only in the very
short run.

Perhaps the most intense struggle between new ideas
and old ideologies will take place over America's political

philosophy, for a fundamental change is taking place in the political values that guide the nation. Since America became a nation, the country has been run on the assumption that the greatest value of all is liberty, which gives people the freedom to "do their own thing," particularly in making money, regardless of how much this freedom deprives others of the same liberty—or of a decent standard of living. Whether liberty means the freedom to squander the country's natural resources or just to go into business for oneself without doing harm to anyone else, it has been a guiding value of mainstream American society.

Today, however, the demand for liberty is often but not always the battle cry of the haves, justifying their right to keep what they have and to get more. Whether liberty is demanded by Southern advocates of states' rights to keep Negroes in their place, or by a property owner to sell his house to any white who wants to buy it, liberty has become the ideology of the more fortunate to be as free as they were in the past to keep the less fortunate in their place.

In the years to come, the have-nots, whether they lack money or autonomy, will increasingly demand the reduction of this form of liberty. Those who ask for more equality are not opposed to liberty per se; in fact, they want more liberty for themselves. Thus they need sufficient equality so that they too can enjoy the liberty now virtually monopolized by the haves.

Many other arguments against equality will be heard in the future. Some will claim that those who want more equality are radicals or outside agitators, seeking to stir up people who would otherwise be content with the way things are. This claim is clearly false, for even when radicals lead the drive for more equality, they can do so only because those who follow them are dissatisfied with the status quo and accept them as leaders.

Another argument is that the demand for more equality will turn America into a society like Sweden, which is thought to be conformist, boring, and suicidal, or even into a gray and regimented society like Russia. But these arguments are false too, for Sweden, which is in some ways still more unequal than America, has a lower suicide rate than Japan, and current events in the communist countries provide considerable evidence that the greater economic equality which some of these countries have achieved does not eliminate the popular desire for freedom and democracy.

But perhaps the most frequently heard argument is that those who are now unequal must earn greater equality. This line of reasoning is taken by those who have had the liberty to achieve their demands, and assume that the same liberty is available to everyone else. This assumption does not hold up, for the major problem of the unequal is precisely that they are not allowed to earn equality; that the barriers of racial discrimination, the inability to obtain a good education, the unavailability of good jobs, the power of college presidents and faculties, and so forth, make it impossible for them to be equal. Those who argue for earning equality are really saying that they want to award it, like charity, to people they define as deserving, but the events in the ghettos and on the campuses have shown convincingly that no one awards equality voluntarily; it has to be wrested from the more-than-equal by political pressure and even by force.

SOME BASIC REQUIREMENTS FOR MORE EQUALITY

Reconciling equality and liberty is not simple, and only a great deal of public debate can determine how it ought to be done. Nor is it simply a matter of giving up a little

liberty for a little equality. There are many kinds of
equality—economic, social, political, and sexual, among
others—and which kinds are most important, how much
equality is needed, and which resources, powers, rights, and
privileges need to be equalized and which need to be allocated on libertarian principles must be debated.

Nevertheless, some of the basic requirements of a more
egalitarian society can be outlined. The American
political-bureaucratic complex must be restructured so
that it will attend to the demands of ordinary citizens and
not just of those best organized to apply maximal political
pressure or make the largest campaign contribution. The
right combination of centralization and citizen control has
to be found to make this complex both democratic and
effective; responsive to majority rule as well as to the rights
of minorities, and at state and local levels as well as at the
federal.

The economy must also be democratized; corporations need to become accountable to consumers and the
general public, and they must be required to shoulder the
social and other indirect costs of their activities. Stock
ownership has to be dispersed, taxes must be made progressive, and subsidies should be used extensively for egalitarian purposes. Unemployment and underemployment have
to be eliminated, and the poverty line raised so that the
gaps between those at the bottom, middle, and top are
reduced and no one earns less than 60 percent of the
median income and eventually no less than 70 percent:
$7,000 for a family of four by today's census figures and
income definition. How high a ceiling on top incomes
and how great a redistribution of wealth are economically
necessary remains to be seen, although both are socially
desirable, and even now there is considerable uproar over
millionaires who pay no taxes. Nevertheless, more income

equality cannot be achieved solely by redistributing the great wealth of the super-rich; redirecting the benefits of future economic growth to the now less-than-equal and imposing higher taxes on the top fifth of the population would also be necessary.

Providing a minimum income of $6,000 or $7,000, which would require public funds for creating new, well-paying jobs, is expensive, although it would also give a tremendous boost to the economy and the tax coffers by releasing the now inhibited purchasing power of the poor. Moreover, America today is sufficiently affluent to afford more income equality. The Gross National Product is currently so high that if it were divided equally among all Americans, a family of four would receive almost $20,000. Part of the GNP must be used for investment, of course, but it would be possible to divide up what economists call Total Personal Income, in which case a family of four would still receive $16,850, over half as much again as the current average family income.[20]

The economically feasible is not always politically achievable, however, and creating a more egalitarian America would arouse considerable political opposition. The more-than-equal would fight any inroads on their privileges, but even the less-than-equal might at first be unenthusiastic, fearful that promises would not be kept and that, as has so often happened in the past, high-sounding policy proposals would subsequently result in legislation once again benefitting the wealthy and powerful. The less-than-equal would soon rally to genuinely egalitarian legislation, but the affluent would still have to be persuaded that money and privilege alone cannot buy happiness in a conflict-ridden society, and that the current American malaise from which they suffer as much as others will disappear only with greater equality. Indeed, I am convinced that what Daniel Bell has called the postindustrial society cannot be held together unless private and public resources are shared sufficiently to give every American a fair chance in the pursuit of liberty.

THE FUTURE OF EQUALITY

Many of the changes called for by the equality revolution will not take place for a generation or more, and how many of them actually come about will depend on at least three factors: the health of the American economy; the reaction of the politically dominant to the demands for equality; and the decision of Middle America as to which side it will be on.

If the economy can move toward full employment and a healthier position in the world economy in the years to come, it will be able to "afford" greater economic equality and the costs of democratizing the corporations and the workplace. If jobs continue to disappear because of automation and foreign competition, however, and if new ones are not created by government, then the poor will be further excluded from what economists call the primary labor market, and democratization will be resisted, even if the unions can bring about some sharing of the work among their members.

But whether or not the economy is healthy, the organized interest groups and the representatives of the affluent who now dominate American politics will try to fight change, and as I suggest in Chapter Two, they may have amassed enough centralized power to succeed. They will need help from more populous groups, however, and the shape of the future will depend in good part on their ability to persuade some of the groups involved in the equality revolution, who want change for themselves but want to hold it back for others, to join them. In the 1972 election, for example, President Nixon was able to persuade a significant number of white Middle Americans, fearful about black demands, to vote for him, although in future years they may again vote for their economic interests as they have in the past.

In fact, since most of the participants in the equality revolution are numerically and politically still quite weak, the fate of that revolution is probably up to Middle America. Although by no means a homogeneous population or a voting bloc, it is the ruling majority in America when it unites, and if large portions of the working and lower middle classes want more democracy and autonomy for themselves, they may be powerful enough to wrest some change from the powers that be. Under certain conditions, such as a severe depression, they might even coalesce with the poor, the black, and other less numerous demanders for more equality, but most likely they will prefer to go it alone. The upper-middle-class demanders of more equality may achieve some of their aims—for example, women— regardless of how Middle America decides to act, but the chances of the poor and the racial minorities outside the upper middle class to obtain more equality look slim.

Still, whatever happens in the years to come, the equality revolution is under way, and however slowly it proceeds and however bitter the struggle between its supporters and opponents, it will continue. It may succeed, partially or completely, but it could also fail, leaving in its wake a level of social and political conflict unlike any that America has ever known.

A PERSONAL NOTE

What I have written so far, I have written as a sociologist, trying to predict the future. But as a citizen, I also believe that most of the now emerging egalitarian trends are desirable, although I do not like what I see in the cards for those most deprived by reasons of income and race. Nevertheless, too many Americans, even among the nonpoor, still lead lives of unnecessary desperation, and the good life today is the monopoly of only a happy few. I think the time has come to revaluate the historic American conception of liberty, but I also think there is no inherent conflict between liberty and equality. The society we must create should provide enough equality to permit everyone the liberty to control his or her own life as much as possible without inflicting undue inequality on others, and how much liberty must be redistributed for this to happen will be the burning issue of the coming generation.[21]

NOTES

This is a combined and revised version of two previously published articles: "The Equality Revolution," *New York Times Magazine,* November 3, 1968, pp. 36–7, 66–76; and "The New Egalitarianism," *Saturday Review,* May 6, 1972, pp. 43–6.

1. The income data are for 1966, and are corrected for nonreporting and underreporting of income. Later data are available, including census data, but they are uncorrected. The wealth data are for 1962. The income data were developed by Joseph Pechman; the wealth data by Edward Budd; both are reported in Letitia Upton and Nancy Lyons, *Basic Facts: Distribution of Personal Income and Wealth in the United States* (Cambridge, Mass.: Cambridge Institute, 1972), tables 2 and 6 respectively. It should be noted, however, that economists are by no means agreed on a definition of income, and every definition will produce somewhat different distributional patterns. Moreover, Richard Titmuss has long argued for a much broader definition of income. See, e.g., Richard Titmuss, *Essays on the Welfare State* (New Haven, Conn.: Yale University Press, 1959), chap. 2; and

S. M. Miller and Pamela Roby, *The Future of Inequality* (New York: Basic Books, 1970), chap. 1.

2. Gabriel Kolko, *Wealth and Power in America* (New York: Praeger Publishers, 1962), p. 51.

3. *Statistical Abstract of the United States, 1971* (Washington, D.C.: Government Printing Office, 1972), table 727.

4. Roger A. Herriott and Herman P. Miller, "Who Paid the Taxes in 1968," paper prepared for the National Industrial Conference Board, March 18, 1971, table 7. See also Joseph A. Pechman, "The Rich, the Poor and the Taxes They Pay," *The Public Interest*, no. 17, Fall 1969, pp. 21–44.

5. Herman P. Miller, *Rich Man, Poor Man* (New York: Thomas Y. Crowell, Co., 1971), p. 16.

6. See, e.g., Pechman, "The Rich, the Poor and the Taxes They Pay."

7. Testimony before the Joint Committee on the Economic Report, January 14, 1972.

8. Alvin Schorr, *Explorations in Social Policy* (New York: Basic Books, 1968), pp. 274–5.

9. W. Lee Hansen and Burton A. Weisbrod, "The Distribution of Costs and Direct Benefits of Public Higher Education, The Case of California," *Journal of Human Resources*, vol. 4 (1969), pp. 176–91. Figures quoted from table 6.

10. David Caplovitz, *The Poor Pay More* (New York: Free Press, 1962).

11. Sam B. Warner, *The Private City: Philadelphia in Three Periods of Its Growth* (Philadelphia: University of Pennsylvania Press, 1968), p. 9.

12. Robert Gallman, "Trends in the Size and Distribution of Wealth in the 19th Century," in Lee Soltow, ed., *Six Papers on the Size Distributions of Wealth and Income* (New York: National Bureau of Economic Research and Columbia University Press, 1969), pp. 22–3.

13. Kolko, *Wealth and Power in America*, table 1; and *Statistical Abstract*, table 504. Between 1910 and 1969, the share of the nation's personal income going to the richest 10 percent declined somewhat, from 34 percent to 29 percent; that of the next richest fifth rose a little, from 22 percent to 28 percent; and that of the middle fifth remained virtually the same, increasing from 15 to 17 percent. The poor just grew poorer, however, for the share of the lowest fifth of the population decreased from 8 percent in 1910 to 4 percent in 1969. It should be noted that Kolko's con-

clusions have been criticized, but there are not enough adequate data to judge properly the recent changes in the distribution of income and wealth during this century.

14. See, e.g., Peter Henle, "Exploring the Distribution of Earned Income," *Monthly Labor Review*, December 1972, pp. 16–27, and his summary of other studies with similar conclusions, *ibid.*, p. 22. A recent *Fortune* article which suggested that inequality was decreasing drew its conclusion from changes in the Gini coefficient, an indicator of over-all national income distribution which measures shares of different income groups in such a way that it can show an increase in equality even if the share of the poorest fifths of the population does not rise. See Sanford Rose, "The Truth About Income Inequality in the U.S.," *Fortune*, December 1972, pp. 90–3.

15. Between 1960 and 1970 the number of people below the poverty line dropped from 22 to 12 percent.

16. In 1970, median family income was $9,867 and the poverty line was set at $3,968.

17. See, e.g., Special Task Force to the Secretary of Health, Education, and Welfare, *Work in America,* (Washington, D.C.: Government Printing Office, 1973); and Harold Sheppard and Neal Herrick, *Where Have All the Robots Gone? Worker Dissent in the Seventies* (New York: Free Press, 1972).

18. R. H. Tawney, *Equality* (New York: Barnes & Noble, 1964), chap. 1, particularly pp. 43, 46.

19. Louis Kelso and Patricia Hetter, *Two-Factor Theory: The Economics of Reality* (New York: Vintage Books, 1967).

20. Bertram Gross, "A Closer Look at Income Distribution," *Social Policy,* vol. 3 (May–June 1972), p. 61.

21. Here again I follow Tawney, *Equality,* chap. 1.

2
The American Malaise

In the summer of 1971, President Nixon, while commenting on the pseudoclassical architecture of American public buildings, went on to suggest that America might be heading for the same fate as ancient Greece and Rome. "As they became wealthy, as they lost their will to live, to improve," he pointed out, "they became subject to the decadence that destroys the civilization. The United States is reaching that period."

Somewhat earlier, Andrew Hacker, an eminent political scientist, wrote a book entitled *The End of the American Era,* and since then other intellectuals and journalists have come to similar pessimistic conclusions. This feeling is not limited to scholars and the media, however, for several polls have reported a widespread mood of malaise about the future of America.

I shall leave it to the classical historians to comment on Mr. Nixon's analysis of the decline of Greece and Rome, but the American malaise has nothing to do with too much affluence, a loss of will to improve, or for that matter, with decadence. Indeed, just the opposite: two decades of American affluence have only reinforced the historic urge of Americans to improve themselves, and the malaise has come about because of the realization that improvement is no longer as easy as it once was. Their will for improvement remains firm, however, and whether America declines or falls apart depends in large part on what kinds of improvements can be made in the years to come, and more specifically, on whether all of the various pressures for improvement can be reconciled, which will in turn require some movement toward a more egalitarian society.

THE DILEMMAS OF RISING EXPECTATIONS

Although America's apparent decline as a world power and the outcome of the war in Indochina have hurt the national pride of some Americans—albeit not of as many as hawkish observers claim—the American malaise is almost entirely domestic in origin. While the president seems to believe that it stems from too much wealth, easy living, and "permissiveness," it has actually developed out of the inability of people to improve their standard of living further. Specifically, it has resulted from two phenomena: the closing of the gap between people's aspirations and their expectations, and a recent widening of the gap between these expectations and their achievement.

While most Americans have always *aspired* to better their standard of living, many more now *expect* to do so, and increasing numbers are *demanding* improvement. The rich, of course, have always been able to treat their aspirations as expectations and to translate them into realizable demands, but until after World War II, most Americans could only dream the American Dream; they were still so busy making ends meet that they could not even dare to expect that this dream could ever become real. One of the crucial changes of the last twenty years has been a new domestic revolution of rising expectations, which has taken place among moderate-income Americans as much as among the poor.

The expectations themselves are not novel; most are still private and have to do with personal and material improvement, although this is less an expression of materialism than a desire for more comfort and convenience. New expectations have emerged, however; people now want more autonomy in their lives and are less willing than in the past to be bossed around by superiors or by antiquated and arbitrary rules, both at work and in the community, and the demand for equal rights that began in the ghettos and the elite universities has spread, more quietly, to many other Americans.

In addition, public expectations are rising; Americans are expecting more from their institutions. Whereas people once only griped among themselves about shoddy goods, they now expect businessmen to cut fewer corners in their products, their pricing policies, and their advertising; and the demand for a cleaner environment has outdistanced recent increases in pollution. Many of these dissatisfactions have been around for a long time, but larger numbers are voicing them than before.

All this has been accompanied by a higher public morality; the existence of hunger and a 6 percent unemployment rate are no longer considered tolerable, and there is somewhat more unhappiness than in the past about conditions in American mental hospitals and prisons—and not only among the prisoners—and about the brutality of war. Although the Vietnam war is hardly the first American war in which atrocities have been committed, it is the first one in which they have become a public issue. In part this is a result of the war's coverage by television and of its unpopularity, but it also reflects the rise in public standards regarding how wars ought to be fought.

Yet perhaps the most significant upturn in expectations concerns the role of government; people now ask for more responsiveness and accountability than before. Moreover, the traditional faith in the ability of private enterprise to run the nation's economy has declined, and people now routinely expect government to be the solver of last resort of America's problems. They look to government to protect and advance their incomes, to provide an inexpensive college education for their children, and to do something about the cost and quality of housing and other services previously left to private enterprise.

When aspirations rise and people begin to hope for a better way of life, they are only hoping; but when expectations are heightened, people become more impatient, more critical of their society when expectations are not realized, and eventually, more active politically. All of these reactions emerged during the 1960s, and show no signs of abating. Of course, the most visible criticism and political action have come from the blacks and other dark-skinned minorities, the educated young, and more recently, educated women, and most Americans have not yet become significantly more active politically. However, protest and demonstration are largely a strategy of minorities, of people who have no other access to government; more populous interest groups can make their demands felt more silently. The fact that they have done so is perhaps best illustrated by the actions of government itself; for example, the Nixon administration's halfhearted resort to quasi-Keynesian economic policies; various restrictions on laissez faire, such as antipollution, car-safety, and other consumer measures; as well as the destruction of many antipoverty programs.

To be sure, the new public expectations are still quite modest in many respects, and public morality has remained tolerant of many kinds of corruption and graft—and of the continued heavy bombing of Indochinese civilians as the war came to an end. Nor is the rise in public expectations as universal as that in private ones. So far, the former have been voiced mainly by the upper middle class—the population that expanded most dramatically as a result of the affluence following World War II—and it is not yet clear how intensively they are felt by the lower middle and working classes of Middle America. Even so, I suspect that among this population, the majority of Americans, expectations are also on the move, and that it is their silent pressure on elected politicians that is responsible for the changes in governmental policy and rhetoric now taking place. Conversely, other Nixon administration policies— such as packing the Supreme Court with conservatives, and intimidating newsmen—are attempts to keep the lid down on a changing America.

EXPECTATIONS AND THE MALAISE

Common sense suggest that the upturn in expectations should have been accompanied by feelings of optimism about the future, but obviously just the reverse is happening. One reason has to do with a psychological difference between aspirations and expectations.

When aspirations rise, people are often optimistic; but when new expectations develop and people assume they can get what they previously only hoped for, they are easily disappointed when expectations are not realized. Aspirations are dreams, but expectations are taken more seriously, and once people expect a better life, they do not resign themselves to a downturn in living conditions. Indeed, when new expectations come into being, people forget the past and evaluate their situation by new standards. For example, blacks and women endured centuries of inequality without much visible protest or even as much private grumbling as their situation justified, but as soon as they began to make some progress toward equality and adjusted their expectations upward, they became impatient with the slowness of their progress. To be sure, expectations can be reduced, as when unemployment strikes, but they are not reduced permanently and are only held in abeyance. Similarly, when expectations are frustrated, they are not given up; instead, people begin to lose faith in their society and question the legitimacy of their polity—as suggested by polls that demonstrate a sharply plummeting amount of trust in government in recent years.

The current American malaise developed originally in the late 1960s when it became apparent that the Vietnam war was causing widespread havoc in the economy, for the galloping inflation and the subsequent recession brought a sudden halt to affluence. In addition, the dissent generated by the war spilled over into other issues, showing many Americans for the first time that the country was seriously divided about many matters.

The malaise also resulted from the new expectations themselves, and might have come about even without the war. The plain fact is that not all the expectations can possibly be achieved, and their very existence has created a variety of economic and political consequences that may have a lasting effect on the character and mood of American life. Even if the difficulties that came in the wake of the Indochina war can be removed, there remains the problem of which and whose expectations can be achieved and whose not. The difficulty—or perhaps the impossibil-

the largest share of the malaise. For one thing, the increasing demand for governmental action to realize these expectations has begun to politicize the entire society, for government decisions now affect more and more of everyday life, and issues that were once considered above politics or nonpolitical are fought out in the political arena. As a result, matters previously decided by fiat, consensus, or the application of traditional values now have to be negotiated, and in many ways America has become a *negotiating society*.

The onset of the negotiating society is perhaps most apparent in the economy; once upon a time, wages were set by management, and later negotiated by management and labor, while prices were left to the not-so-tender mercies of the market and later to corporate setters of administered prices. But today, all are often matters of public policy, to be negotiated in Washington. Political issues were usually decided by a handful of politicians in the White House and the Congress with the advice and consent of a few lobbyists, while today, many more lobbyists and even constituents have to be consulted. In the social sphere, decisions were reached on the basis of long-accepted if not always agreed-upon values: whites expected to tell blacks how to behave, teachers dominated their students, and businessmen decided what their customers wanted—perhaps with an assist from market research—and answered complaints with a feeble form letter.

Needless to say, many—perhaps most—decisions are still made unilaterally, but this gets a little harder all the time. Parents continue to try to boss their children, and teachers their students, but some students now take their teachers to court and others go on vandalistic rampages when negotiations break down. If whites are to dominate blacks politically, they now must elect a racist politician, although even he is likely to have to negotiate with the black community once he is elected. Old rules—such as those that denied public employees the right to strike, Southern blacks to run for office, or enlisted men to question officers' orders—have fallen by the wayside, and once-autocratic institutions must negotiate with the people they controlled in the past.

Perhaps the best illustration of all this is in the handling of the Vietnam war. President Johnson and his colleagues thought they could make decisions about escalating the war in the traditional manner, consulting only the military and political experts, and LBJ lost his job partly because he failed to touch base with enough of his constituents. And because he made so many unilateral decisions, some Americans felt that they were being deliberately deceived even when this was not his intent.

Of course, some of LBJ's actions in the war, like Nixon's after him, were deceptive, and since then the Watergate scandal has convinced many more people that government leaders are not to be trusted. But whether or not they resort to deception, today's politicians are in a difficult position, for politicization and the demand for negotiation bring political conflict out in the open, raising popular awareness of the conflict and increasing the dissatisfaction of those on the losing end.

In addition, when people have higher expectations and want their interests represented politically, more interests and interest groups must be considered in every political decision, so that decisions are harder to reach, particularly those that can satisfy everybody. The indecision and inaction that come with the greater demand for participation also add to the malaise, and evoke memories of allegedly good old days when decision-making was easier.

The greater demands placed on government have also

led to the realization that government cannot do as much as is expected of it. Although the New Deal nurtured the belief that social problems could be solved through federal action, Nathan Glazer, Daniel Patrick Moynihan, and others have pointed out that government is better at appropriating funds than at delivering services to the intended recipients. Often, the federal government's failure is a result of sabotage of its programs by local governments or power-holders—sometimes reflecting the wishes of the over-all community, often only those of a powerful few— and federal funds are occasionally diverted by city halls to other purposes, so that the true abilities of the federal government to implement "social policy" have not yet been properly tested. Of course, federal social policies alone cannot do away with the pathologies associated with poverty, but they could reduce poverty. In any case, whatever the causes, the limits of governmental effectiveness also help to frustrate the achievement of higher expectations.

The final and perhaps most important reason for the malaise is that the new expectations are developing in and running head on against the old economic and political system, which cannot really deal with them. America is, after all, still a very unequal society in which wealth, income, and power are highly centralized; 1 percent of the people own a third of the nation's total assets, and the two hundred largest corporations do a majority of the nation's business. Government is equally centralized; it is more responsive to its own bureaucracies and to the best-funded and most highly organized interest groups than to other citizens; more to businessmen than to consumers; and more to suppliers of military hardware than to advocates of peaceful software.

This state of affairs is less a result of conspiracy than of past arrangements; it reflects an older society in which popular expectations were lower and few people expected either the economy or the government to meet their wishes and needs. Consequently, they remained politically inactive, and both the economy and the government responded mainly to groups that already had high expectations and were organized to implement them, developing centralized decision-making routines they are now not always able or willing to change.

Many corporations, once having freed themselves from the market, can administer prices and raise their own capital, so that stockholders and customers are largely excluded from their decision-making process. The excluded are currently trying to intervene in this process, but the barriers against them are formidable, and many corporations are still trying to keep them out—and to keep from having to negotiate—by saturating the media with commercials attesting to their democratic and public-spirited character.

Governmental decision-making routines are in much the same boat; over the last few decades, government has increasingly freed itself from direct accountability, by bypassing Congress, and by the isolation of the bureaucracies—and the increasingly powerful White House staff—from the political process. Here, too, the excluded are trying to breach the walls, and although governmental walls are more porous than corporate ones, new points of view still have difficulty in getting themselves heard when and where it counts.

Ralph Nader and others are struggling to make the corporate and governmental apparatuses more accountable to the general public, and their success so far could not have been achieved without the favorable public climate in which they are working. At the same time, greater success is held back in part by some traditional public attitudes that support the existing centralization. For one thing, many people do not care how public decisions are made so long as these decisions benefit them. Others still believe sufficiently in laissez faire to doubt the desirability of public intervention in the affairs of business, although this belief is far weaker than it was only a few years ago. Similarly, despite the fact that government affects people's everyday lives to a much greater extent than ever before, many people continue to see it as their enemy, which demands taxes for wasteful expenditures that do not benefit them and that they would rather spend privately.

Still, there is enough public dissatisfaction with centralization to create a feeling among many people that they are powerless and increasingly so, that they cannot bring about change even if they want to—and this too contributes to the malaise. To some extent, their judgment is accurate; as bureaucracies become more important and corporations larger, the centers of power are harder to reach, and of course, as more people want a voice, each voice must, by simple arithmetic, become less powerful. Nevertheless, some of the feelings of powerlessness are themselves a consequence of higher expectations. When people did not demand power, they did not realize how powerless they were, and only now that they want it do they feel that they are powerless—and unhappy.

THE NEW CONSERVATISM

The rise in expectations has also been accompanied by reactions that are often described as a new wave of conservatism in American life, but are actually attempts by economic and other interest groups opposed to the realization of these expectations to nip them in the bud.

These reactions take several forms, the main one being a counsel for more modest expectations and a return to traditional values which themselves call for modest expectations and for less negotiation. Conservative politicians, supported by a new breed of conservative intellectuals, argue that too many people are becoming overly "permissive" and are also asking too much from government, that wages are high enough and productivity not, and that welfare recipients are too scornful of the traditional work ethic. President Nixon said much the same thing when he argued that Greece and Rome fell because they were too affluent and grew lazy and decadent, the implication being that if people were less wealthy, they would work harder and America would not decline.

Whatever the specifics of these arguments, their proponents are saying that expectations must be reduced to uphold the social order and keep America from falling apart, and that the traditional values that once restrained people from making too many demands should be revived. Many of the people who put forth these ideas are themselves quite affluent, both in income and in power, and having achieved their own expectations are now asking less affluent people to tighten their belts. Even so, they are not likely to persuade the people for whom their appeals are intended, for rising expectations are not easily reversed.

A variant of the appeal for reducing expectations is a new celebration of American gradualism, with conservatives pointing out that progress is being made and that modest goals achieved gradually are more appropriate than radical ones involving militant political action. They also call for more optimism about the future, and some intellectuals have even attacked radical critiques of American society as anti-American. Of course, progress is being made; for example, some blacks are entering the middle class and in some respects are duplicating the gradualist process by which European immigrants made it into the American mainstream. Still, the political implication that blacks should duplicate the patience of the immigrants and put their faith in "progress" is not justified. Even if radical change is unlikely, gradualism is not automatic, and depends, as do most other forms of change, on political and economic pressure. Moreover, people whose expectations have just risen and who have therefore just become visibly impatient cannot be expected to abide by a gradualist process endured by past populations, particularly when those populations had a considerably lower level of expectations.

I do not want to suggest that the demand for conservatism comes only from the affluent; it also comes from some moderate-income Americans who exaggerate and resent the modest rise in income and power experienced by the poor and the blacks during the 1960s, and from all groups used to exercising relatively unilateral authority who resent the demand for negotiation and are unhappy with the concurrent politicization of their members. Professionals complain about the lack of respect now paid them by clients who want both better service and more accountability, and union leaders are upset by wildcat strikes and young workers who question union cooperation with management on many issues.

Likewise, adults are complaining about the rising expectations of the young. Although the so-called generation gap has come about mainly because many educated young people are advocating economic and social values that are diametrically opposed to those of upper-class and Middle America, many adults, rich and poor, are also angry because these young people seem to be having it easier all the time and obtaining more of the pleasures of life to boot. In part this is the traditional hostility of moderate-income adults toward affluent youth, but it is fueled further by complaints about drug use and sexual freedom.

The new ways in which young people are pursuing pleasure are presumably what the president had in mind when he warned that decadence might destroy American civilization, and adults have always offered such warnings when young people rejected their values. Still, there is no evidence that America is becoming decadent; marijuana does not appear to lead its users into a life of sloth and fantasy as much as alcohol, and the liberalization of sexual values has not brought about a decline in public morality or social order. In fact, the same students who now sleep together more readily are also the most insistent pressure group for a higher morality in public life, whereas revolutionaries are frequently sexual puritans, for revolution is an all-encompassing passion that drives out sex and the pursuit of pleasure generally.

Actually, sex is one area of life in which high expectations can be achieved painlessly, which is all the more frustrating to people whose nonsexual expectations are not being realized. Moreover, while economic and political changes usually have far-reaching consequences, changes in sexual standards do not. People with traditional moral beliefs are upset, of course, but the fact that stag films once shown only in private men's clubs and on veterans' posts can now be seen in public movie houses has not been accompanied by any noticeable increase in sexual pathology, and that fewer brides are now virgins has not reduced their marriageability, since virginity stopped being an asset when marriage ceased to be a economic transaction for parents. To be sure, sexual liberalism has reduced the power of parents to treat their adolescents as presexual beings and thus as children, but it has not increased the economic or political power of young people, which is why the new eroticism can ultimately be tolerated more easily than the proclivity of eighteen-year-olds to demonstrate.

Finally, the frustration of expectations has produced a wave of nostalgia, a renewed celebration of the good old days when traditional values were still intact, consensus was the informal law of the land, and politicization and negotiation had not yet emerged to escalate political conflict. For example, the nostalgia for the 1940s that appeared shortly after the start of the malaise was no mere accident, for that decade was romanticized as a period free from political conflict and a polluting technology, dominated by a popular and just war, and characterized by innocuous love songs and movies in which sex—and politics—never reared their heads. Needless to say, the real 1940s were not that pleasant, but then societies tend to remember only the pleasant aspects of the past. The wheeling and dealing that accompanied the War of Independence and the creation of the Republic are long since forgotten, and in an era of militant racial and ethnic minorities, the Lower East Side of the early twentieth century is now falsely remembered as a cheerful neighborhood of cohesive families exchanging recipes for ethnic dishes on tenement stoops.

THE MALAISE AND EQUALITY

The future of the American malaise depends largely on the outcome of the clash between rising expectations and an economic and political system still geared to a society of lower expectations, and that outcome is impossible to predict. If the new expectations are as widespread and intensely felt as I have suggested, one could argue that the status quo cannot long persist and that the system must change, by becoming more responsive and accountable, and by bringing about at least some redistribution of income and power to satisfy those with rising expectations. On the other hand, it is also possible that the centralization of the economy and the government has gone so far that corporate and political leaders have sufficient control over the available resources and power to ward off large-scale change.

I am inclined to think that in the long run the system will change, because it has always changed just enough to survive, although the change will be far slower and less complete than the new expectations demand. Meanwhile, only three guesses about the future can be made with any assurance. First, expectations will continue to rise—or at least will not decrease—and the voices of those who advocate reducing expectations and returning to traditional values will become louder. Second, and more important, political conflict over the distribution of income and power—that is, who gets what—will increase, and though almost all political issues have ultimately revolved around this question, people will be more aware of it, which may in turn affect their political attitudes and actions.

The distribution of income has already been placed on the public agenda by Senators Fred Harris and George McGovern, both of whom mentioned the inequality of the current distribution during their ill-fated campaigns for the presidency. Senator McGovern called for the elimination of tax loopholes and preferences that benefit mostly the very rich, and even though he was defeated, the proposals he made will undoubtedly be revived in one form or another, as I will argue further in Chapter Six.

The distribution of power has always been on the public agenda, but since power is less visible than money, its redistribution has remained more an inchoate yearning than a concrete political demand, except among blacks and advocates of community control. Still, there is enough dissatisfaction with centralized bureaucracies to suggest that demands for other kinds of power redistribution may arise. In fact, President Nixon's attempt to redistribute power from the federal bureaucracies to state and local ones through revenue-sharing is partly a response to public dissatisfaction, even though it is intended to transfer power from liberal federal officials to conservative state and local ones. Moreover, once enough people realize that his scheme will not be responsive to "the people"—that is, the Middle Americans he is wooing—but will only enlarge the less competent bureaucracies at the state and local levels, they may set off a backlash that might ultimately lead to demands for making bureaucracies more responsive to their constituencies. As I noted earlier, however, this backlash will not by itself resolve the difficult problem of determining the priority with which various constituencies are to be responded to, and which are to be left out when all cannot be satisfied.

Third, even if policies for redistributing wealth, income, and power become politically viable, it is quite possible that the poor, the black, and other minorities will not benefit from them, for as I suggested in Chapter One, the Middle American majority will be concerned mainly with achieving its own demands. The probable result will be more unrest, particularly in the ghettos, and more crime in middle-class neighborhoods, and this will make life harder, particularly in the cities—but then, life will get harder for everybody. Even if good economic times return and even if there is some redistribution of income and power, the struggle over whose expectations will be met and whose not and the continuing politicization of society will increase the amount and intensity of public conflict. And since Americans are not really used to resolving distributional questions or living with political conflict, the current malaise may become permanent, at least until these questions are resolved.

Ending the Malaise

Nevertheless, the phenomena I have described and the predictions I have ventured do not justify the conclusion that America is declining, falling, or falling apart. Societies do not decline because they are too rich, as President Nixon would have it, but because their people are unable to find a fair way of dividing up the available wealth and power.

The past twenty years have seen a rise in the expectations of the poor and the Middle Americans, who are now beginning to demand a larger share of the pie of wealth and power. This is hardly a sign of decline or decadence, but of vitality and the very will to improve that Mr. Nixon thinks is disappearing. And if America adapts to the rise in expectations, it is even a sign that justifies some optimism about the future. Of course, if Middle America tries to obtain its share of the pie by further squeezing the poor and if the poor fight back, then it is possible that America will one day fall apart from internal strife, and not in its cities alone. But if both obtain a larger share—and mainly from the rich and from the economic growth that lies ahead—then America may become a somewhat more egalitarian society than it has been in the past. To some, particularly among the rich, this may signify the end of America, but it is only the end of an America that should have disappeared earlier.

NOTE

This is a slightly revised version of an article with the same title which appeared in *The New York Times Magazine*, February 6, 1972, pp. 16–17, 24–34.

II
THE POSSIBILITIES
AND PROBLEMS
OF MORE EQUALITY

INTRODUCTION

Despite the title of this part of the book, the essays in it pay more attention to the problems of equality than to its possibilities, in part because its possibilities depend on how the problems connected with it are solved. Unlike the skeptics and critics I discussed in the preface, I believe that the problems are solvable, although not so easily in the real world as in a book. Still, the essays here often aim to suggest possible solutions.

Part II opens on a more general and theoretical note, however. Chapter Three starts with a definition of equality, and argues that among the many kinds, economic and political equality are most important. The body of the chapter is about some major problems of equality, such as the conflict between equality and the maintenance of work and other incentives, which actually represent possible contradictions between equality and other social goals, for example, economic efficiency.

Chapter Four looks at the problems of equality from a somewhat different perspective. Though concerned mainly with poverty, this essay suggests that both poverty and inequality exist in part because they have positive functions— or uses or benefits—for other sectors of society, and that as long as they are functional, they are not likely to disappear. Poverty is useful, for example, because the poor constitute a pool of people who can be forced to take the dirty jobs in the economy that no one else will take, and at low wages. Egalitarian policy-making requires either finding egalitarian substitutes for those functions which are necessary to society, or a reorganization of society so that inequality can be eliminated because it is no longer useful or beneficial to anyone. In theory, at least, "dirty" work could be equalized by paying people higher wages for it than for "clean" work. In practice, policy-oriented solutions are much harder to find, partly because poverty and inequality have many functions—not only economic but social, psychological, cultural, and political ones— and because many of these functions cannot be substituted for, except at great cost to their present beneficiaries. Moreover, it is difficult to conceive of social conditions under which the benefits of inequality they receive do not outweigh the costs they must pay. With respect to poverty, one could perhaps argue that if class conflict escalates to the point that even the rich cannot escape it and the costs of protecting the more affluent from the poor outweigh the costs of an effective anti-poverty program, poverty will no longer be functional. However, I consider this possibility unlikely.

In Chapter Five, the emphasis is on political inequality, particularly of the economic and racial groups that are numerical minorities and thus likely to be outvoted in a democracy based on majority rule whenever a majority refuses their demands. Given the widespread antagonism toward the poor and the black, such a majority is easily put together, and the poor and the black are thus perhaps doomed to be permanently outvoted minorities. The essay asks, therefore, whether majority rule is inherently necessary to democracy, and makes a number of proposals that would result in greater equality for these minorities.

Chapter Six is not only the final essay in Part II, but insofar as Part III of the book is devoted to research proposals and utopian speculation, it is also the final chapter of the book for those interested in egalitarian policy issues. It may also be the most immediately relevant essay in the book, for it suggests that political pressures for income redistribution may develop in the foreseeable future, drawing here on the conclusions reached in Part I. The chapter proposes tax reform through the adoption of the Credit Income Tax, a new way of levying taxes which Senator McGovern had in mind during the 1972 presidential campaign when he proposed giving $1,000 to every person. Actually, the Credit Income Tax is only an improved version of the Negative Income Tax, and it "gives" money (in the form of tax credit) only to poor, near-poor, and some moderate-income people. The main purpose of the essay is to discuss the major economic and social effects of income redistribution through the Credit Income Tax. Applying some of the conclusions about the fate of work and investment incentives under equality described in Chapter Three, I argue that tax reform would not reduce these incentives, and that the fears of economic decline and chaos voiced after Senator McGovern made his proposal are largely groundless. Conversely, income redistribution would not only improve the lot of all Americans now earning less than the median income, but to the extent that it eliminated poverty, it would also reduce at least some of the crime and pathology associated with poverty as well as some of the tension and conflict between the haves and have-nots in American society. Nevertheless, there will be considerable political opposition to even the minimal amount of income redistribution envisaged by the Credit Income Tax proposals discussed here, although I believe that when moderate-income Americans, who after all constitute a political majority in this country, realize that they will benefit from the institution of the Credit Income Tax, income redistribution may become politically feasible.

3
Some Problems of Equality

More equality may be morally desirable or politically necessary, but few human societies and no modern ones have so far achieved a significant degree of equality, and the reasons are not difficult to find. Societies that have no use for private property, such as nomadic and hunting tribes, find it easy to be egalitarian, but societies that enable individuals to collect such property do not. Moreover, in societies marked by scarcity, or at least by felt scarcity, social life is often—though not always—competitive, for families and other groups each struggle to overcome scarcity for themselves, rather than cooperating and sharing the available resources. Still, there are poor societies and poor groups within more affluent societies who do share, particularly when opportunities for escaping poverty are so meager that no one is tempted to resort to competition.

Affluent societies can afford to be more egalitarian, but

even so, the achievement of more equality is blocked by a number of problems that have to be solved, and as realistically and pragmatically as any other social problem. In this chapter, I want to discuss some of these problems: the conflict between equality and upward mobility; the maintenance of incentives to work and invest when unequal rewards are reduced; the allocation of those resources which are so scarce that they cannot be allocated in an egalitarian fashion; and the conflict between equality and authority. Before turning to these problems, however, I want to begin with the definitional problem: What is equality, and what is a reasonable definition of equality for contemporary America?

What Is Equality?[1]

The term *equality* is, by itself, so general that it is virtually meaningless without further qualification. In its common-sense meaning, equality is sameness or uniformity, but it can be discussed only by specifying (1) its outcome, (2) the resource or right that is to be made uniform, and (3) its subjects, the persons or roles so affected. And if more equality is the aim, the degree to which resources or rights are to be made uniform must also be specified.

OUTCOMES OF EQUALITY

Three alternative outcomes of equality are generally considered: equality of opportunity, equality of treatment, and equality of results. Insofar as America has had an egalitarian tradition, it has been for equality of opportunity: the right of every person to get ahead without hindrance by reason of race, sex, age, and parental social position. This principle has little to do with equality, however; it is a libertarian principle which allows everyone the same liberty to strive for success, and because it is libertarian, it has not produced a great deal of equality of results. People who start their lives at a disadvantage rarely benefit significantly from equality of opportunity because, unless they are outstandingly superior in skills or in upward-mobility techniques, they can never catch up with the more fortunate, and most disadvantaged people never even get access to the supposedly equal opportunity. A few poor children may eventually end up in the prestigious professions, but many do not finish high school. Equality of opportunity is also an asocial principle, because it ignores the many invisible and cumulative hindrances in the way of the disadvantaged; in fact, unless the children of the poor are taken from their parents at birth and brought up in middle-class homes, most are condemned to inequality of opportunity.

Equality of treatment can be interpreted in two ways. On the one hand, it means treating people as roughly equal in impersonal social interactions, such as shopping, without regard to their social status, which is very important to low-status people and distinguishes America from Europe, where different classes are treated unequally across the board.[2] On the other hand, it means providing people with the same resources regardless of their current resources or socio-economic position; used in this sense, equality of treatment suffers from the same drawback as equality of opportunity, for to treat the disadvantaged uniformly with the advantaged will only perpetuate their disadvantage. Even in the courts, which pride themselves on equality of treatment before the law, the defendant who can afford only a poor or overworked lawyer will not often obtain equal treatment from the judge. Consequently, the only truly egalitarian principle is equality of results, which may require unequal opportunity or treatment for the initially disadvantaged so that they eventually wind up equal in resources or rights.

Equality of results can produce sameness; when everyone is equal with respect to a given resource, every person has the same amount of that resource, and if all resources were equalized, everyone would be uniform on all counts. Such uniformity is neither desirable nor achievable; a society in which everyone had an equal amount of the same resources would probably be deathly boring, but in any case it is not achievable. For one thing, human beings differ in many characteristics, and not all these differences can be erased by an equality of resources. For another, in a society with a division of labor, sameness is impossible because people fill so many different roles. Consequently, one must consider what kinds of equality are desirable and achievable.

EQUALITY OF RESOURCES

Many resources can potentially be equalized: income, power, occupational skills, cultural skills, status, prestige, and respect, among others. I would argue that insofar as respect and prestige are subjective states, resources that people award each other largely on the basis of their own feelings, they cannot easily be equalized. Moreover, these feelings in turn reflect the differences in roles produced by the division of labor, and so do two other resources, occupational skills and status. If the modern division of labor is to be retained, a society without differences in occupational skills, status, and prestige is impossible. Cultural skills might well be equalized more by giving everyone the same liberal arts education, though not necessarily the same vocational one, but occupational and other differences would still produce cultural variety, and besides, cultural homogeneity would be undesirable. Consequently,

I would argue that income and power are the most important resources to be considered for equalization.

As I interpret the egalitarian ideal, equality of income and power does not mean that every person would wind up with the same consumer goods and services and the same political roles; rather, that everyone would have equal shares of these resources but not be required to use them in the same way. Thus, in a completely egalitarian society, everyone should receive the same income, but ought to be free to spend it as he or she wishes. This would ensure the basic freedom to choose different goods, services, and lifestyles, thus encouraging cultural diversity, although it would also enable people to spend their income in order to obtain more money, which could create new inequalities. Similarly, everyone ought to have the same amount of power, but ought to be free to exert it—or not exert it—as he or she wishes, although those who chose to exert it could then become more powerful than the rest. A society that was completely egalitarian in allocating income and power would therefore have to find ways of discouraging new inequalities from arising.

COMPLETE EQUALITY VERSUS MORE EQUALITY

A completely egalitarian society strikes me as so utopian as to be beyond policy-oriented discussion. If all incomes were equal, it is doubtful that the most unpleasant and taxing jobs would be filled, and if all power were equalized, it is doubtful that any decisions could be made and any public activities could proceed. Moreover, such a society would need to be heavily regimented to prevent new inequalities from arising, and it would have to be static, straining toward a totally egalitarian end-state above all else. The major defect of complete equality is the defect of all single-value conceptions: if equality is the all-encompassing goal, then all other goals, regardless of their desirability or necessity, become lower in priority, and no society can function by pursuing one goal above all others. Some of the critics of equality have made this point, hoping thereby to end any discussion of equality, but complete equality is a spurious issue. The real issue, at least from the point of view of pragmatic social policy, is more equality, that is, how much present levels of inequality of income and power should be reduced. Putting it this way does not detract from the importance of equality as a goal, but it makes it possible to ask how much equality is feasible, and at what costs for the achievement of other goals. What degree of income equality is compatible with the division of labor, with filling unpleasant jobs, and with economic efficiency generally? What degree of political equality can be achieved in a large heterogeneous society that must inevitably be run by bureaucracies, and by political leaders who must represent—and thus in some ways be more unequal than—the citizens in whose names they act?

These are fundamental questions for egalitarian thought, and I can answer them only in very general terms. No person should have less income than is necessary to pay for the minimal goods and services considered essential for the American standard of living—for the standard package, as Lee Rainwater puts it—or than is necessary for him or her to be a fully participating member of American society. No one has yet computed the size of this minimum, although a long series of Gallup polls asking respondents how much they need to get along in their present community have shown that this minimum is about 70 percent of the median income, except that the poor, whose wants are more modest, have generally said they could get by with an income equivalent to 60 percent of that median.[3] Consequently, more equality means, at least for me, that no person should have an income of less than 60 to 70 percent of the society's median, however income is defined; or rather, of the median income for a particular position in the life-cycle, and in the case of families, of the median income by family size.

Conversely, the income ceiling ought to be determined on two other grounds. One is John Rawls's well-argued principle that above-the-median inequality is desirable only when it helps to reduce below-the-median inequality.[4] The other ground is pragmatic economic efficiency: What is the lowest maximum at which people continue to be willing to do unpleasant or highly responsible work or take needed investment and other risks? Both criteria can only be evaluated by economic analysis, and it may turn out that there ought to be no ceiling; that given the small number of multimillionaires in American society, more would be lost by reducing people's ability to strive for the maximum than by expropriating most of the income of a few millionaires—although this does not negate the desirability and urgency of requiring the rich to pay higher taxes than anyone else. A 100 percent tax on income beyond a certain point may be undesirable, but that does not rule out a 75 to 80 percent tax. And similar questions must be raised about minimum and maximum amounts of wealth: What should be done with the undistributed profit and other wealth of the large corporations, and with the old fortunes that still play such a central role in the American economy? How much wealth may be passed on to the next generation through inheritance?

With respect to political power, the achievement of more equality through the setting of floors and ceilings is impossible, since power is neither quantifiable nor an individual attribute; it usually attaches to groups and roles.

I suppose one can establish some general thresholds and ceilings; no person should be so powerless that he or she has no control whatsoever over his or her own life, and no person should be so powerful that he or she can force others to do his or her bidding without taking these others into account. It is possible to establish total electoral equality, giving every person one vote and requiring that person to vote or to cast a blank ballot, but this is only one kind of political equality and not the most important kind by any means. If campaign expenditures were nationalized, as I suggested earlier, then the power to influence political candidates would be removed from the rich, but it would not necessarily be equalized; it might reside in those politicians and bureaucrats who oversee the expenditure of campaign funds. In addition, a corporate manager who can decide how many people will be hired or fired and where a plant will be located will always have more influence with a president, congressman, or mayor than one of his employees. This may not even be undesirable, as long as the manager is elected by or is otherwise responsive to his or her constituents, but these should include not only the company's stockholders but also its employees, who must have some degree of worker control, its customers, and the general public insofar as it is affected by company decisions. A manager's influence must be an outcome of group decisions.

Because power is primarily a group attribute, more political equality in fact requires the internal democratization of all groups, so that their members can have a greater say about the actions of their leaders. This means, in practice, that all groups exerting some power ought to be led by elected leaders, chosen by their members and by those nonmembers whose lives are affected by that group, including not only corporations but also governmental agencies and voluntary associations. But more political equality also requires some equalization of power between groups, so that consumers do not always lose out to producers, or the poor to the rich. All this probably means that the federal government must become more powerful than all other groups if only to be able to implement greater equality among them. While this is undeniably a disadvantage of a more egalitarian society, it seems unavoidable, and the net benefits in greater equality for the large number will outweigh the costs of a more centralized government, provided of course that this government is restricted in its own efforts to amass more power by a pervasive system of checks and balances and by frequent elections.

THE SUBJECTS OF EQUALITY

The subjects of equality, the people or groups for whom more equality is desirable, are, in the most general sense, those who are now unequal, which I would interpret to mean unequal with respect to income and power. This should not be a matter of great debate, but opponents of "affirmative action" and quotas have recently argued, and with considerable passion, that in America resources should be allocated to people on their individual merits and not on the basis of their membership in some group, particularly one that is defined by ascription rather than achievement. Consequently, they argue, it is wrong to suggest that X percent of jobs in a firm or university ought to be reserved for blacks or Y percent to women, particularly if this means that people who are not qualified will be hired. Aside from the fact that in all firms or universities, unqualified people are sometimes hired because they have political influence or are in the right place at the right time, the distinction between ascribed and achieved characteristics strikes me as irrelevant. To be sure, women differ from men with respect to their role in procreation, but equality of income and power, and occupational qualifications, have nothing to do with procreation, and the major ascribed characteristic of women is therefore irrelevant, as is skin color in the case of blacks and other racial minorities.

Needless to say, unqualified people should not be hired, but qualification must be measured by performance and not by credentials. Most advocates of meritocracy fail to make this distinction, and in fact do not even consider that merit can be defined in different ways. For example, defenders of meritocracy in the university argue that university standards would be lowered by hiring unqualified colleagues, but qualification is almost always defined by credentials, by having a Ph.D. or the right kind of Ph.D., and not by classroom performance. The university—or rather, the graduate school—illustrates the limited relevance of credentials, for although it trains its graduate students to become researchers, most Ph.D.s, whatever their field, do little research after graduation and perform almost entirely as teachers. Therefore, if merit is to be defined in terms of performance, the relevant qualifications are those of teaching performance in the classroom, not the possession of a researcher's credentials, for no one has yet proved that Ph.D.s are better teachers than M.A.s. To be sure, some teachers should be hired for their research performance so that research will be conducted, and some teaching is better done by researchers, particularly that involving training and practice in research. But until the defenders of meritocracy broaden their definition of merit and judge it in terms of performance, they are only defending the right to have *their* credentials serve as the prime indicator of qualification.

Some people will be deficient even on the basis of

performance, although such a judgment should not be made until on-the-job training is provided for them. This training should be possible for almost any job, even in a university, and in many cases, it need take only a fraction of the time now required by prejob education. People who fail to perform adequately after such training ought not be allowed to stay in a meritocratic institution such as the university, but until merit is measured by performance, a university cannot even claim to be meritocratic.

Equality between occupations is probably impossible in a society based on a complicated division of labor, but more equality is desirable both between and within occupations, for over 90 percent of the jobs paying $15,000 or more a year are held by white males. Altering this statistic may take some time, and it must proceed more quickly in those occupations where total employment is rising, but even though more equality of results must be accompanied by equality of performance, this cannot be achieved by limiting women and blacks to inferior jobs. Moreover, when race and sex have been used for over a century as criteria for not hiring people, it is hypocritical to argue that they should not be used as criteria for hiring because this would be "reverse discrimination." In terms of equality of results, this simply means the continuation of the traditional discrimination, albeit for a different reason.

To be sure, if faculty with poorer credentials are hired or students with a poorer educational background are admitted to a university, "standards" will decline. The new faculty may teach at lower levels of abstraction, and the new students may sometimes be unable to comprehend what the incumbent faculty is teaching; and insofar as the newcomers can affect the teaching program or the intellectual climate, the levels of both will be lowered, at least from the perspective of the incumbents. But for the newcomers, who will have a chance to teach and learn at higher intellectual levels than before, the standards will be raised, and the real issue is whose perspectives are to be favored.

This issue is not limited to the university or to meritocracies generally; it comes up in changing neighborhoods and is generic to implementing more equality, for it requires a comparison of the benefits (for the newcomers) and the costs (for the incumbents) of egalitarian policies. In theory, a society could decide that the benefits are worth the costs and that incumbents will have to learn to adjust to what is for them a decline in standards and also in status. In practice, however, the decision is arrived at politically, sometimes favoring the newcomers, as in most changing neighborhoods, where they pay inflated prices for their rise in status; sometimes favoring the incumbents, as seems to be the case at least in private high-status universities. Sometimes, compromise solutions are possible, such as providing remedial training to the newcomers or segregating them so that the incumbents can operate at their accustomed level; but when such compromises are not possible, the group with greater political influence tends to win out. In theory, egalitarian policy would have to side with the newcomers, unless the incumbents can prove their argument that their contribution to society is so important that the rights of newcomers must be abridged; but while that argument is politically persuasive, it is difficult to prove. And if the institution is publicly supported, it is particularly dubious for incumbents to suggest that prior occupancy justifies permanent control over standards.

EQUALITY AND EQUITY

Finally, one must distinguish between the goals of equality and those of equity. Equality has to do with sameness of results, while equity, or fairness, concerns the relationship between one person's work or other effort and the reward for that effort, and another person's effort and reward. Thus, inequity occurs when one person works harder than another but gets less reward, and equity would presumably equalize rewards on the basis of similar effort. As such it differs from equality of results, which ignores the concept of effort and assumes that everyone is entitled to equal rewards regardless of effort, or rather, that everyone will exert equal effort because of equal results. Such an assumption is not realistic, however, for if equality of results were guaranteed, some people might work less hard.

This consideration alone makes equity an important concept. Also, many Americans are probably more concerned with equity than with equality; they want society to be fair, not equal. The continued sanctity of the work ethic suggests that they are reluctant to provide equality of results to those people who, for one reason or another, do not exert productive effort by working, even if their unemployment is not their own fault. Thus, greater equity could produce more inequality, for people who did not work would get less, although if equity were measured also by the effort taken to find work, then equality of results would also be an equitable solution.

The major problem with the concept of equity therefore centers around the idea and measurement of effort. If effort is defined in terms of the outcome of exerted effort, equity would have more income going to those who are more productive or more important to the economy or to society. The problem is how to define "productive" and "important"; surely the loan shark plays a productive role in the economy, but his rewards are not determined by equity. Importance is even harder to ascertain because it requires answering the question, Important for what? While the theoretical physicist may be important in pushing forward the frontiers of knowledge, the garbage man is important in guaranteeing everyone's good health, including that of the physicist. Equity judgments thus require agreement about the major values of the society; in a society that was not able or willing to stress scientific innovation, presumably the garbage man would get a higher salary. Of course, equity can also be defined in terms of the amount of training required for a particular effort, as it tends to be in America, so that by this criterion the physicist would earn more than the garbage man; but there would be little equity to this arrangement if the physicist had been supported by government stipends all through his or her training period and did not make sacrifices to achieve that training for which equity demanded that he or she be recompensed later. In real life, physicists earn more than garbage men because their work is considered more important by those who make public decisions, and because physicists have, until recently, been a scarce resource whereas the potential supply of garbage men far outweighs the demand; but these criteria have little to do with equity.

If equity is defined in terms of the willingness to exert effort, however—as it ought to be—then incomes should be based on that exertion, and the shirker, whether physicist or garbage man, should earn less. The problem here is the measurement of exertion. Effort so defined is difficult to measure, for it is ultimately a personal attribute, and operational indicators of effort, physical or mental, are hard to find and to compare. Moreover, some kinds of work require more effort than others, so that equity would mean inequality for people whose jobs required less effort. Thus, the physicist with a light teaching load who did not research might earn considerably less than the garbage man, although this would by no means be unreasonable since the former was obviously shirking. Also, equity is a subjective concept, because what people deem to be fair depends on their own evaluation of their effort as compared with that of others, and few people would downgrade their own exertions. It is perhaps possible to develop operational indicators of exertion to be used for public policy, such as number of hours worked, and equity would then demand, as it does now, that people who work longer hours receive more pay.

Here, equity and equality would coincide, for while everyone would earn the same income in a completely egalitarian society, equity could be provided by reducing the number of hours worked, particularly in jobs requiring great exertion. However, an egalitarian society—unlike an equitable one—must find methods of controlling shirking. In theory, shirkers could be punished with job loss or income reduction, as they are in an existing society, but in practice this would award a great deal of power to those people who decided who was shirking, with obvious dangers of regimentation and the possibility that people who did not get along with the decision-maker would be punished as shirkers. In this respect, equity is more desirable than equality.

Another problem of equity is that it requires many more judgments about what is equitable, whereas equality of results is more easily administered. Of course, from another perspective, this problem is a virtue; equity takes individual conditions into consideration more than equality. Much depends here on how equality is defined and what a society deems to be equal. For example, equity would demand that a family with three children receive more income than a childless couple, but while a completely egalitarian society might make the same decision, it could also argue that if people have equal incomes, they can then decide to spend it on children or on whatever childless couples spend their income on instead. This, however, assumes that the society is not interested in encouraging fertility.

Equality and equity both have virtues and vices, but equality is deficient without equity, and equity is deficient without equality. Equity requires some degree of equality, for inequality is unfair. Conversely, more equality would itself bring about greater equity, and once major inequalities were removed, individual cases that might require some new inequalities in the name of equity could then be dealt with more easily.

EQUALITY AND INDIVIDUAL STRIVING

One major problem that egalitarian thinkers must solve is the conflict between more equality and people's striving for more income, status, power, and the like. This is particularly true in America, for the history of America is a history of people striving for more resources, and of an economy and polity that have encouraged such striving. To be sure, one can find political and legislative decisions in American history that resulted in greater equality—or upward mobility—for the disadvantaged, such as the abolition of slavery, the Homestead Act, the establishment of land-grant colleges, the federal income tax, the legitimation of unions, and public housing; and the American economy has in its unplanned ways provided greater equality, as during the first half of the twentieth century for parts of the working class. Yet little of this legislation and even less of the economic trend were propelled by egalitarian notions, for America has not had an egalitarian tradition. In fact, even many who now participate in what I described in Chapter One as the equality revolution are not deliberately seeking equality; they too want the right to have more, whether of income or of power.

The idea of equality is questioned because it denies the desirability of upward mobility. Moreover, greater equality would generate some downward mobility among the especially advantaged, and the pains of downward mobility are always hard to bear, particularly in America.

Perhaps even more important, the universality of the belief in upward mobility creates considerable opposition to any egalitarian policy that appears to give people, particularly at the lower end of the socio-economic ladder, something for nothing, or more specifically, an income grant without their working for it. This reaction is often ascribed to the existence of a work ethic, but actually, it reflects the unwillingness of people who are striving to reward anyone who is not also striving. At the level of theory, this is not a serious problem, for it requires only that income redistribution be achieved at least in part by putting people to work rather than simply by giving them an income grant. In practice, however, it requires an economy of full employment and a massive governmental job-creation program to provide jobs to the now unemployed, underemployed, and underpaid.

The striving for upward mobility has also generated an individualist ethos in America which creates further problems for the achievement of more equality, for individualism accentuates diversity, lack of social cohesion, and perhaps most important, distrust of group and governmental action. A more egalitarian society inevitably requires more governmental regulation, but few people now trust government sufficiently to put their fate into its hands. Middle America's opposition to Senator McGovern's tax-reform proposals was engendered in part by its feeling that government could not be trusted to bring about reforms that would benefit it. Of course, this reaction stems partly from the legitimate feeling in Middle America that it is not an equal partner in government; if more moderate-income people held high governmental positions it might feel sufficient trust in government to allow reform to proceed.

However, egalitarian legislation would also require greater trust in government from the advantaged, for even if they could be forced politically to make the sacrifices that more equality would exact from them, their own political reaction would be affected by the feeling that such sacrifice should provide them with some benefits as well, if only psychological or social ones. For example, some rich people might be somewhat more willing to accept tax reform if they knew that the outcome would be more social peace and less conflict-creating upward mobility—or "uppity behavior"—on the part of those lower in the socioeconomic hierarchy.

Given the diversity and upward striving that mark American life, however, it is unlikely that the rich can obtain any assurance that if they gave up some of their economic resources, they would obtain something else in return. Nor is this feeling unjustified, for it is doubtful that compensatory sacrifices on the part of the beneficiaries of more equality would be forthcoming. Indeed, income redistribution might only encourage more upward mobility on their part; as some of their expectations were realized, new ones would emerge.

In other words, more equality is not likely to come about easily and peaceably in an individualistic, heterogeneous, and noncohesive society where there is little trust between groups—or, among these groups, in the government. As long as the homogeneity and cohesion prerequisite to trust are not available, people who stand to lose from more equality will not consider their losses legitimate, and they will argue that as long as everyone else uses the social system, the economy, and the polity for their own personal advancement, they are entitled to act similarly.

It is of course possible to argue, as the Chinese and Cuban Communists have done, that once a more egalitarian society is created, a change in human nature will take place so that people will feel they have a common stake in the enterprise and will thus have enough trust in each other to make sacrifices. From all accounts, this argument seems to be working in the People's Republic of China at present, reinforced no doubt by the vast cultural machinery that exists to change national symbols and the content of education, as well as by the expropriation and killing of the old advantaged classes.

Even so, it is also possible to doubt that the public altruism which tends to follow in the wake of egalitarian revolutions will persist, even among those who have benefitted from it. The history of the Israeli *kibbutzim* suggests that the members of these egalitarian communities were quite altruistic in the early years, but once the survival of the community had been assured—and thus their own as well—and some surplus income became available, they rediscovered their egos and began to want some individual choice in their lives. The same process is likely to take place eventually in China as well, despite all governmental efforts to prevent it. Governments can control people's behavior, at least for a time, but they cannot control people's aspirations, and once these return to some individualistic goals, they are quickly translated into political demands. The decline of altruism need not spell an end to equality; when the economy is productive, it can satisfy consumer demand without creating competitive individualism. The affluent *kibbutzim* have acceded to demands for a higher standard of individual living as soon as they could do so for everybody—for example, by providing every family with its own TV set and by giving everyone a small allowance to indulge personal tastes. When egalitarian revolutions fail, however, or fail to improve the lot of the average citizen—as seems to have been the case in much of Eastern Europe and in Cuba—then the altruism engendered by the revolution disappears much more quickly, and people resort to traditional competitive ways to find satisfaction.

The Chinese, Israeli, Eastern European, and Cuban examples are not directly relevant to America, for America is so dedicated to individual striving that even a temporary altruism is inconceivable. Indeed, if America ever accomplished a more egalitarian income redistribution, most Americans would look for new ways of adding to their income. Suburban flower gardens would be replanted with vegetables so that people could spend the money so saved for other goods, carpenters would exchange their services with automobile repairmen, do-it-yourself operations would decimate those paid-for services that people can perform for themselves, and various forms of barter would become popular. Much the same has happened in some socialist countries, for the tendency of equality to go against the social and psychological grain of individual striving is not limited to America.

These observations do not negate the desirability of more equality or even its feasibility, but they require a realistic conception of its scope and limits. That conception suggests, first, the sociological impossibility of a completely egalitarian society, for as long as people have egos, they will strive for differentiation and some inequality. Second, it requires the assumption that people's aspirations will continue to combine self-interest, about private matters and the public good, with some limited altruism, and that they will therefore continue to want more resources, consumer goods, and other appurtenances of comfort or "bourgeois culture."

These observations also reinforce my earlier point that the proper egalitarian goal is to reduce inequality of income and power without ending people's freedom to use their income and power as they deem best. Moreover, it might be worth considering for a society pursuing more income equality to encourage certain kinds of inequality at the same time, as long as these did not impinge on income equality: for example, by enhancing status competition, particularly in nonwork pursuits, and by offering more honors and other symbolic rewards. Of course, status remains in the eye of the beholder, and a society cannot long offer symbolic rewards unless these are treated as rewards rather than as cheap substitutes for money; but it is probably true that if income redistribution discourages striving for high income, people who need to strive will find other material or nonmaterial objectives.

EQUALITY AND INCENTIVES

A second problem of equality stems directly from the first: given the human dedication to individual striving, whether people will continue to work and invest if more equality restricts economic rewards for their efforts, and whether they will find incentives to contribute to the economic and social growth and functioning of their society.

The evidence from the Israeli *kibbutzim* suggests that in societies without individual property (except for basic personal necessities and minimal luxuries), income equality will not depress such incentives and people will continue to do the necessary work, although if the opportunity arises, they will shun the physically most unpleasant manual jobs and the emotionally most taxing nonmanual jobs, such as decision-making positions, particularly those requiring unpleasant political negotiations with their fellow *kibbutz* members.[5] As a result, many *kibbutzim* have begun to hire outside workers for manual labor, despite the prohibition against wage labor in *kibbutz* ideology. However, the strong social control exertable in small, bounded communities like the *kibbutz* still makes it possible to persuade members to take on the political tasks reserved to members, or to punish them for shirking their duty.

When the opportunity to obtain private property is available, completely egalitarian income policies seem to depress incentives, so that several Eastern European socialist countries have now begun to raise wages for skilled workers and managers in order to increase productivity, though whether this strategy is actually effective remains to be seen. Conversely, Sweden has recently reduced the income differential between the upper middle and working classes, and a few countries, notably Israel, have never developed extreme forms of this differential, in both instances without significant effect on productivity.

America has operated on a fairly but not unusually high income differential between kinds of workers, and policies aimed at greater equality would have to reduce this differential by putting floors and ceilings on either before-tax or after-tax incomes. As I suggested earlier, the latter policy is preferable. Greater equalization of incomes through tax reform would be politically more desirable and bureaucratically more feasible than equalization of wages and salaries; it would be less likely to shackle the urge for individual striving and upward mobility, and it would have a less depressing effect on status-seeking.

Under tax reform, an executive with a $50,000 salary might not take home $20,000 more than a colleague earning $30,000, but he or she would still retain whatever symbolic rewards and status go with the $20,000 dollar difference in before-tax income.

A more radical and in the end more egalitarian approach would be to redefine work so as to eliminate the need for jobs paying very high or very low salaries and wages.[6] Greater income equality without any depressing effect on incentive would result if $50,000 jobs were divided into two each paying half that amount and if very low-wage jobs could be automated or otherwise eliminated. Neither alternative is always possible, of course, and if an executive position is split in two, the job of the next higher executive is complicated because then two persons must report to him or her, but job redefinition is particularly relevant to a society in which, as in ours, job scarcity is becoming a problem.

Even with some degree of job redefinition, three specific questions must be raised about the impact of more equality on incentives. First, would poor people be willing to work if they could obtain a minimum-income grant without working? Second, would the more affluent work as hard if income redistribution levied higher taxes on them? And third, would investors continue to take risks if their expected profits were reduced by income redistribution?

THE INCENTIVE TO WORK

Most economic theorists generally argue that economic rationality would dictate a negative answer to all three questions, for conventional economic theory assumes that people do not like to work, will not work if they can receive an income grant instead, will work less energetically if their net income declines, and will not invest if their after-tax profits are insufficient. Unfortunately, neither economists nor sociologists have done sufficient empirical research to test these assumptions, but the vast literature of occupational sociology suggests that, at least with respect to work, human beings are not purely economic persons, acting only on the basis of economic rationality, and that social motives, pressures, and rewards exist which are perhaps as important as economic rewards.

In America, as in most modern societies, work is the most widely accepted indicator of social usefulness and thus the best allocator of individual respect and identity; and social usefulness, respect, and identity appear to be basic and universal human needs. People need to work not just to make a living but also to feel useful, and if they cannot work, they soon begin to feel useless, even to themselves, and to fall into depression.[7] Moreover, the need to work seems to be built into the modern psyche; few people are socially and emotionally self-reliant enough to enjoy a life of leisure, and even the very rich take on civic projects.

These reactions are felt by the poor as well as the rich, and studies of welfare recipients have shown not only that many work when they can, but that they want to work and would prefer work to welfare. This is even true of mothers who are household heads and might be expected to stay home.[8] The reasons for their desire to work are not difficult to find. Aside from wanting to get out from under the stigma of being on the dole, poor people want to maximize their income as much as anyone else so that they can obtain Rainwater's standard package. Even nonstigmatizing income grants seem to have a similar effect; judging from the early findings of the Office of Economic Opportunity's experiments, giving people extra money in the form of a Negative Income Tax spurs their desire to work and to look for better jobs. Consequently, the conventional belief that added income depresses work incentive among the poor is inaccurate; just the reverse is true, and income grants vitalize the work incentive, while lack of money forces people to concentrate on day-to-day survival, so that they lack the energy, morale, and above all self-confidence to look for work.

However, if the labor market is such that the only jobs available to poor people are badly paid, insecure, and dirty, then they may stop working if they can obtain a similar and more secure income from an income grant. Thus, any egalitarian policy that included a minimum-income grant would have to expect some people to walk away from or stop taking the worst jobs. This is by no means undesirable, for it might encourage the abolition of some of these jobs, but it would in turn raise production costs and thus prices, and new jobs would need to be created for people in low-wage industries that could not continue to exist as a result.

As for the affluent, income redistribution should not reduce work incentives; studies by Lester Thurow for the labor force in general and by George Break and Thomas Sanders among samples of middle- and high-income employees show that people work harder and longer after their taxes go up.[9] Consequently, the $50,000 executive who was taking home less money would not stop working; in fact, he or she would probably try to find a better-paying job. At the very highest salary levels, other job attributes such as fringe benefits, status, and power would presumably come into play, so that candidates for the presidency of General Motors would still step forward even if the job paid less in after-tax income than it does at present.

However, when people cannot work harder or longer,

as in jobs that do not allow for overtime, or when they cannot obtain better-paying jobs, some incentives might decline. And while many self-employed businessmen, doctors, and other professionals and employed workers who can make extra money through moonlighting could work longer hours, they might not do so if they were already putting in long hours and if income redistribution took away most of their extra income. If more equality interfered with badly needed productivity, it would obviously have to be counteracted by increased incentives, and ultimately, government would have to make a decision as to how badly the lost productivity was needed. This could not help but increase the power of government, but this is an unavoidable cost of more equality, although it is no greater a cost than when an undemocratic corporation makes the same decision. Moreover, other policy alternatives are also possible. If income redistribution led doctors to take on fewer patients and their loss of productivity had to be corrected, it is possible to conceive of substitute incentives, such as special honors for devotion to duty; and more realistically, of other policies, such as recruiting more doctors. The government might set up more medical schools, shorten the period of medical education, and raise stipends and salaries for medical students and interns, reducing the sacrifices that come with medical training so as to recruit more doctors. In effect, the government would be raising potential doctors' incomes early in their career while income redistribution reduced their later incomes, a trade-off that would not only reduce inequality but might also help to alleviate the shortage of doctors.

Conversely, the kinds of people with whom the critics of equality are most concerned, that is, intellectuals, artists, and scientists, would work just as hard, and the level of culture and science would not be affected by more equality. Such people are striving for recognition and prestige, not

for more money, and although they do not reject the economic rewards that come with fame, their incentives to
work would be affected more by policies that attempted to
reduce the prestige of high culture. For example, someone
with artistic ability would be less likely to become a serious
painter if museums were required to devote 75 percent of
their exhibits to popular art, but he or she would not be
deflected by a lower income. The serious painter might
lose some sales if redistribution cut heavily into the incomes of rich art buyers—and most art buyers are rich—
but this too would not seriously affect the incentives of
people to become serious painters. While it is true that the
vitality of high culture requires some inequalities, which
raises the question whether a vital high culture is more
desirable than greater equality, high culture needs the inequality that comes with meritocracy more than inequality
of income and wealth.

Older people might not work so hard if they could not
pass on as much of their fortune to their children, but
while no society can totally suppress people's desire to hand
down the fruits of their labor to their children, the incentive loss among the elderly rich is not always a critical
loss as far as productivity is concerned, and it would encourage greater equality of wealth. Besides, as better health
care increases the longevity and health of the old so that
old age becomes more enjoyable, and as the children of the
rich rebel or drop out in larger numbers, the incentive to
work hard in order to build a family dynasty and achieve
immortality by passing on an inheritance will decline in
any case.

Judging by evidence from socialist economies, it is
possible that an over-all reduction of economic incentives
might depress the general level of work effort and set off
a tendency to take it easier on the job. This tendency is

already present even in nonsocialist societies; evidently, once people have a moderate amount of economic and job security, they no longer work quite as hard as when they were driven by hunger. More income equality might exacerbate this tendency, and it is probably true that a more egalitarian society would be less productive, which is one reason greater equality is more feasible in an affluent society than in one that must go all out to maximize productivity. Even so, the decline of productivity would depend on the nature of the job. Where most of the work was done by machines, productivity would not be affected significantly by the workers' inclination to take things easier; the principal decline of productivity would take place in labor-intensive manufacturing and in the secondary and tertiary retail and service occupations. Consequently, greater income equality would require compensatory devices to make work more satisfying in order to recoup lost productivity: for example, job redefinition, which is already being tried on today's assembly lines, and some degree of worker control over the policies of their firm. Where job redefinition was impossible, employees, employers, and government would have to decide whether the productivity loss could be afforded, or whether incentives or sanctions to reduce shirking would have to be set up.

THE INCENTIVE TO INVEST

The incentive to invest and to take risks with one's money is more governed by rational economic motives than work, but even investment is a social process, and an individual's investment decisions are affected by those of others. Assuming that the present structure of the economy were retained but that income redistribution reduced the

net income from investment, fewer people would invest
and many might decide to spend their money for consumer
goods instead. Among the very rich, however, who after
all are the most important investors, there are limits to
consumption, and ultimately they would have to invest
their money. They might not be happy about a lower
after-tax profit, but as long as every other investor was in
the same boat, their relative deprivation would be mini-
mized and they would continue their investment role,
seeking to do better than everyone else.

The stock market might not survive, at least in its
present form, under conditions of greater income equality,
but then it is a minor source of investment capital even
today. Philip Stern has estimated that only 5 percent of
the corporate capital requirement is now raised in the
stock market.[10] Most investment is carried on by the
corporations themselves, either from their own funds or
from money sources outside the stock market. Moreover,
their incentive to invest would not be significantly reduced
in a more egalitarian economy, because they need to continue to grow and to prevent their competitors from obtaining a larger share of the market. Among small and
family-owned firms, more economic equality might reduce
investment incentives, but among large oligopolistic corporations, this seems highly unlikely, although there might
be some reluctance to make extremely risky investments.
Where such investments are needed, more unequal rewards
would have to be provided, and small and family-owned
firms might have to be unequally rewarded as well if they
were not to be reduced in number even further.

If more income equality resulted in a decline in investment incentives and thus in investment itself, this
would have to be compensated for by lower corporate taxes
or by a higher level of government investment. Some

corporations might find it difficult to continue operating and would have to be nationalized; others might have to be nationalized to make control over their funds and their operations more egalitarian. If government were sufficiently democratic to make socially more desirable investment decisions than private industry, this might be all to the good. As far as the generation of investment capital is concerned, however, such measures may not be necessary. If more economic equality were achieved through the creation of jobs, then the new consumer demand, the new savings, and the various other externalities generated by a full-employment economy would stimulate investment to make up for what had been lost by the decreased incentive of the rich.

EQUALITY AND SCARCE RESOURCES

The problem of incentives is ultimately only part of a larger problem with which egalitarians must deal: how to allocate resources which are so scarce that they cannot be or should not be allocated in an egalitarian fashion. The two problems are related in the sense that sometimes higher incentives—and more unequal rewards—may be necessary to increase scarce resources, particularly when it is politically impossible to do so through public investment.

If resources are so scarce that they do not suffice for everybody, then they cannot be allocated equally, and some cannot be increased either by raising incentives or by public investment. Two kinds of scarce resources can be distinguished here: divisible and indivisible. Income falls into the first category, for although total societal income is scarce insofar as it is always less than what people want, income could be divided equally. Some opponents of income equality argue that income equality would create inequality of satisfaction, for people who need more money to satisfy their needs would be deprived. Therefore, they suggest that satisfaction should be equalized rather than income, by determining the marginal utility of satisfaction for everyone and then giving more to the persons who are hardest to satisfy. These suggestions almost always end up in support of the status quo, because they assume, a priori, that the rich and the highly cultured are harder to satisfy than the poor.[11] Moreover, since satisfaction is virtually impossible to measure, this approach is of doubtful validity, whereas if income is equalized, every person is able to maximize his or her individual satisfactions by deciding how to spend that income.

Other resources are not divisible, however. For example, despite Picasso's prolific talent, there are not enough Picasso originals for every person in the world or even in America. In this case, there are two egalitarian solutions. First, if incomes were equal, then some people could decide to spend it for a Picasso original and skimp on other expenditures, while those who felt less urgent about owning an original could buy a reproduction. Second, some of the Picasso originals could be placed in public ownership and exhibited in museums so that everyone could at least enjoy them on a temporary basis.

These solutions would not work for other indivisible resources, such as heart transplants. Since hearts usable for transplanting and doctors trained to transplant them are scarce, at least at present, not every heart patient can obtain one. While it is possible to argue that with complete income equality, transplant operations could be allocated through the market, giving people the right to decide whether to spend their income for a transplant, this would be a brutal right, for it would force them to decide how much their own survival was worth. Besides, given the high value placed on survival, most people would choose to pay the market price, and yet there might still not be enough hearts and doctors to satisfy the demand. In theory, it would be possible to draw lots, in which case every heart patient's opportunity to obtain the operation would be equal, but in terms of an equality of results, there is no way by which this resource could be divided equally.

Another indivisible resource is education. Even in a completely egalitarian society which provides a free college education to every citizen, some schools will be better than others and only a few can be among the best. Although the distribution of such schools need not be as pyramid-like as at present—and would not be if students came from roughly the same socio-economic background—still, even a totally egalitarian society could have only a few colleges of Ivy League quality, and inequality would be perpetrated on those who were excluded from such schools.

A society with complete economic equality could probably solve this problem on a market basis, by raising the cost of attending Ivy League schools so as to enroll only those who were willing to pay the price, although in such a society, Ivy League schools might not be as desirable as they are now because the economic incentives that influence a youngster's decision to go to an Ivy League school would probably be less, since higher income could not be obtained through a better education. Consequently, a market solution would be far less brutal than in the case of the heart transplant. Drawing students by lot would not be effective, however, for the quality of the Ivy League schools is created in part by their ability to attract the brightest students, and random selection would reduce the schools' quality.

If scarce resources are indivisible and cannot be allocated in an egalitarian fashion, then other criteria must be used. Inequality has always served the easily applied function of rationing such resources by making them available only to the more affluent or powerful or both. The traditional solution has been to identify other goals as more important than equality, so that, for example, Ivy League schools are rationed by sending only the brightest students to them, with the justification that society needs the highly trained professionals and intellectuals they produce.

This raises the question, Which goals are more important than equality, and how is this importance to be determined and by whom? The prime criterion often suggested here is societal need, and the advocates of meritocracy argue that a postindustrial society needs highly trained intellectuals and professionals so badly that this criterion even justifies the maintenance of present inequalities, as in the number of female and black intellectuals and professionals. Societal need, however, is difficult to determine, if only because society is not a homogeneous social unit and agreement on its needs is not likely to be obtained. If the very survival of society were at stake, such agreement would probably be obtainable because everyone values survival highly, but if societal survival were assured, some people might argue that needs served by professionals and intellectuals, such as advancing knowledge, maintaining a high place in the international scientific competition, or creating the technological and other innovations that would maximize the Gross National Product, were less urgent than other goals, such as distributing the existing innovations to more people, or increasing the level of public and individual health.

Functional analysts of inequality argue that the prime criterion is functional importance; Davis and Moore, for example, have suggested that society rations its scarce resources—and personnel—by rewarding those of greatest importance more than anyone else.[12] The difficulty with this criterion is much the same as with the first: as long as different things are important to different people, who is to decide what is functionally important to society? Moreover, even if there is agreement on what is important, those who are benefitted by this agreement may then use their benefits to consolidate their income and power further, thus discouraging any attempts to reduce these if their importance has decreased. For example, because survival and good health are so highly valued by most people, doctors are important in almost every society. In many societies, their very importance encourages public policy to increase the supply of doctors, but in America, it has allowed doctors to obtain a monopoly over the provision of health services, and thus not only to gain extraordinarily high rewards but to use those rewards to oppose any diminution of their monopoly power.

Davis and Moore and some other functionalists look to the market and the social process in general to decide what resources are most needed or most important. Daniel Bell has observed similarly that "there may be good market reasons for insisting that the wages of a physician and dentist be greater than those of a nurse or dental technician, for if each cost the patient roughly the same . . . no one would want to use a nurse or dental technician, even in small matters."[13] Leaving these decisions up to the market or the social process is viable when everyone is roughly equal, but otherwise, those with the greatest income and power will obviously obtain most of the scarcest resources. Bell's observation is thus most relevant if incomes are equal enough to allow everyone to make the choice of doctor or nurse through the market. One can also argue, however, that if doctors and nurses charged the same price, the former would have more freedom of choice among patients, and at the same time the supply of nurses would increase sufficiently so that any patient who wanted to be assured of certain and immediate treatment would go to the nurse. In both cases, time, another scarce resource, would be allocated in a fair manner. But it is also possible that people who preferred the doctor to the nurse would try to bribe him or her so as to be admitted to treatment, thus setting up a black-market situation. The latter possibility is likely in an egalitarian society of self-interested human beings, and insofar as the legitimacy and morale of a society are impaired by the existence of black markets, maintaining wage and price differentials may be desirable, particularly when more income equality can be obtained through other means.

The basic problem can be posed most baldly by returning to the transplant example. If not enough transplant operations can be performed to meet the demand, who should receive them? Philosophers have grappled with this type of question for ages, but it is ultimately a political question that society as a whole must answer; in fact, it is the basic political question. To decide how scarce and indivisible resources should be allocated is also to decide what goals and whose goals are of highest priority in the society. Even in an egalitarian society, equality can never be the only goal, and the desirability of other goals must constantly be measured against that of equality. Goals can only be determined politically, however, and if a society is democratic and politically as egalitarian as possible, the political process must be used to let the citizenry or its representatives make this determination.[14]

There is one egalitarian answer to this question: Rawls's previously mentioned principle that inequality is justified when it leads to greater equality of the disadvantaged. Thus, if it could be proved that restricting the

Ivy League schools to the brightest students would ultimately help the poor and near-poor, this might well be the
most egalitarian allocation principle that could be devised.
Whether or not it could be proved is another matter. For
example, Ivy League graduates could be required to pursue
careers that would help the disadvantaged—for example,
as teachers—but it might be that the disadvantaged would
be helped more if these schools were reserved for the most
creative businessmen who, in improving economic productivity for everyone, would raise the incomes of the poor as
well. One virtue of the Rawlsian principle is its empirical
testability; presumably, sophisticated economic analysis
could determine what inegalitarian policies are most effective in reducing the plight of the disadvantaged.

Equality and Authority

In a more egalitarian society, questions such as the allocation of scarce resources must obviously be politicized and
political decisions must be made about the goals for which
such resources will be allocated. In a nonegalitarian society, these decisions are made by the holders of power
in terms of the goals they deem most desirable, either for
themselves or for society or both, which may simplify the
decision-making process and avoid difficult questions about
societal goals, whatever the shortcomings from the egalitarian perspective.

Greater politicization brings up yet another problem,
the conflict between equality and authority, for authority,
whether at work or in the polity, gives unequal power—
and may give unequal resources—to its wielders.[15] Complete political equality means the elimination of most
authority and thus requires direct democracy, but while

this is appropriate to the utopian scenarios to be discussed in Chapter Eight, it is of little relevance to a large heterogeneous modern society.

Authority is intrinsic to the division of labor and representative democracy, and if the goal is more equality, authority need not be eliminated but only harnessed. As I suggested earlier in the chapter, positions of authority can be democratized by making them elective as much as possible, by requiring wielders of authority to take all their constituents into account, and by enabling these constituents to participate in the decision-making process when that is feasible, or to have access to authority figures and final control or veto power over them when that is not possible. (Ways of achieving more equality of participation, access, and control are discussed in Chapter Eight, pp. 206–210.)

Another difficult problem is restricting wielders of authority to the roles for which authority is required, and discouraging them from using the power that goes with authority to obtain special privileges. Here one must distinguish privileges necessary to the wielding of authority from those not necessary. For example, if executives or professors are in short supply so that their time is scarce, they should presumably not be required to do their own typing, although with job redefinition, there might be enough executives and professors with enough time to do their own typing, enabling people who did not want to be typists to seek other jobs. Similarly, if executives had no other symbols of authority, they might be allowed to have large offices or executive bathrooms, although a more egalitarian society should be able to invent less costly symbols than space. Conversely, wielders of authority do not need to be able to send their children to the best schools in order to perform their own role, although in a more egalitarian society where authority was democratized, their role would become a more difficult one, which in turn might require special incentives to attract candidates. This, however, remains an empirical question; certainly New York City in 1973 had no difficulty in attracting candidates for the mayoralty even though the job appears highly undesirable, at least to nonpolitical outsiders. But if candidates for positions of authority do not appear on the scene, then unequal incentives will be necessary, and as long as such incentives cannot be passed on to the next generation, they do not appear to be great cause for alarm.

CONCLUSION

This chapter has discussed what I consider some of the most important problems of equality, but obviously there are others. For example, I have not dealt with the conflict between equality and status. This omission was deliberate, for with economic equality, the grossest status differences would be eliminated. Even with complete economic equality, people would continue to seek status differentials, but as long as such differentials could not create major new inequalities, they ought to be treated as inevitable and not necessarily undesirable givens of human behavior. I have also left out what might be called "voluntary inequality," which occurs when people award special privileges to individuals whom they consider highly for one reason or another, for example, movie stars whom they enjoy seeing or artists and writers whom they venerate because they speak meaningfully to the human condition. Such individuals perform emotionally and intellectually significant functions in every society, but their high status depends almost entirely on their ability to serve these functions, and when they stop doing so, their fame declines quickly. Also, they are individuals and cannot by themselves alter the structure of society in an inegalitarian direction. With some degree of economic equality, their wealth will be reduced in any case, but given the needs and ambitions that drive them, they will still seek public acclaim, and judging from the societies that even now pay their movie stars much less than ours, the supply of candidates for voluntary inequality of this kind will not evaporate.

NOTES

This essay was written especially for this volume.

1. This section of the paper draws extensively on R. H. Tawney, *Equality* (New York: Barnes & Noble, 1964), particularly chaps. 1 and 2.
2. The importance of this kind of equal treatment is discussed in Lee Rainwater, *What Money Buys* (New York: Basic Books, forthcoming), chap. 9.
3. Lee Rainwater, "A Decent Standard of Living: From Subsistence to Membership," unpublished paper, and *What Money Buys.*
4. John Rawls, *A Theory of Justice* (Cambridge, Mass.: Harvard University Press, 1971).
5. Ephraim Yuchtman, "Reward Distribution and Work Role Attractiveness in the Kibbutz," *American Sociological Review,* vol. 37 (October 1972), pp. 581–96.
6. The idea of job redefinition as a redistributive device was proposed by Lester Thurow and Robert E. B. Lucas, *The American Distribution of Income: A Structural Problem* (Washington, D.C.: Government Printing Office, 1972).
7. Marie Jahoda, Paul Lazarsfeld, and Hans Zeisel, *Marienthal: The Sociography of an Unemployed Community* (Chicago: Aldine Publishing Co., 1971).
8. Leonard Goodwin, *Do the Poor Want to Work?* (Washington, D.C.: Brookings Institution, 1972).

9. Lester Thurow, *The Impact of Taxes on the American Economy* (New York: Praeger Publishers, 1971); George Break, "Income Taxes and Incentives to Work," *American Economic Review,* vol. 47 (September 1957), pp. 529–49; and Thomas Sanders, *Effect of Taxation on Executives* (Cambridge, Mass.: Harvard University Press, 1951).

10. Reported in Michael Harrington, "Ideally, We Should Abolish Every Subsidy in the Internal Revenue Code," *Saturday Review,* October 21, 1972, p. 49.

11. See, e.g., Bertrand de Jouvenel, "The Ethics of Redistribution," in Edward C. Budd, ed., *Inequality and Poverty* (New York: W. W. Norton & Co., 1967), pp. 6–13.

12. Kingsley Davis and Wilbert Moore, "Some Principles of Social Stratification," *American Sociological Review,* vol. 10 (April 1945), pp. 242–9. See also Bernard Barber, *Social Stratification* (New York: Harcourt, Brace & Co., 1957).

13. Daniel Bell, "Meritocracy and Equality," *The Public Interest,* no. 29 (Fall 1972), pp. 29–68, quotation at p. 65.

14. In an egalitarian society, equality is by definition no longer a political goal, since consensus about its desirability has been reached. In a nonegalitarian society, however, equality is as political as any other goal. This argument is elaborated in Herbert J. Gans, "Equality and the Public Interest," *Journal of the American Institute of Planners,* vol. 39 (January 1973), pp. 3, 10–12.

15. Sociologists have long debated whether social differentiation, as between those with authority and those without it, must entail social stratification, but I am here concerned with differentiation only insofar as it results in stratification. When authority does not bring extra resources to its wielder, it is not a source of inequality, but such a situation is rare. On this topic, see Davis and Moore, "Some Principles of Social Stratification"; Melvin M. Tumin, "On Inequality," and Wilbert Moore, "Rejoinder," *American Sociological Review,* vol. 28 (February 1963), pp. 19–28.

4
The Positive Functions
of Poverty and Inequality

The preceding chapter examined some problems of equality from the perspective of society as a whole, but still other problems are identified when one looks at the functions—or benefits—that inequality provides for specific sectors of society. This chapter examines such functions of poverty and, in a concluding section, of inequality, taking off from the Mertonian analysis of the functions of the urban political machine.

In analyzing the persistence of the political machine, Robert K. Merton wrote that because "we should ordinarily . . . expect persistent social patterns and social structures to perform positive functions which are at the time not adequately fulfilled by other existing patterns and structures . . . perhaps this publicly maligned organization is, under present conditions, satisfying basic latent functions."[1] He pointed out how the machine provided central authority to get things done when a decentralized local government could not act, humanized the services of the impersonal bureaucracy for fearful citizens, offered concrete help (rather than law or justice) to the poor, and otherwise performed services needed or demanded by many people but considered unconventional or even illegal by formal public agencies.

This chapter is not concerned with the political machine, however, but with poverty, a social phenomenon as maligned as and far more persistent than the machine. Consequently, there may be some merit in applying functional analysis to poverty, to ask whether it too has positive functions that explain its persistence. Since functional analysis has itself taken on a maligned status among some American sociologists, a secondary purpose of this chapter is to ask whether it is still a useful approach.[2]

THE NATURE OF FUNCTIONS

Merton defines functions as "those observed consequences which make for the adaptation or adjustment of a given system," and dysfunctions as "those observed consequences which lessen the adaptation or adjustment of the system."[3] This definition does not specify the nature or scope of the system, but elsewhere in his classic paper, "Manifest and Latent Functions," Merton indicates that social system is not a synonym for society, and that systems vary in size, requiring a functional analysis "to consider a *range* of units for which the item [or social phenomenon—H.G.] has designated consequences: individuals in diverse statuses, subgroups, the larger social system and cultural systems."[4]

In discussing the functions of poverty, I shall identify functions for *groups* and *aggregates,* specifically, interest groups, socio-economic classes, and other population aggregates—for example, those with shared values or similar statuses. This definitional approach is based on the assumption that almost every social system—and of course every society—is composed of groups or aggregates with different interests and values, so that, as Merton puts it, "items may be functional for some individuals and subgroups and dysfunctional for others."[5] Indeed, frequently one group's functions are another group's dysfunctions.[6] For example, the political machine analyzed by Merton was functional for the working-class and business interests of the city but dysfunctional for many middle-class and reform interests. Consequently, functions are defined as those observed consequences which are positive *as judged by the values of the group under analysis;* dysfunctions, as those which are negative by these values.[7] Because functions benefit the group in question and dysfunctions hurt it, I shall also describe functions and dysfunctions in the language of economic planning and systems analysis, as benefits and costs.[8]

Identifying functions and dysfunctions for groups and aggregates rather than systems reduces the possibility that what is functional for one group in a multigroup system will be seen as functional for the whole system, making it more difficult, for example, to suggest that a given phenomenon is functional for a corporation or political regime when it may in fact be functional only for its officers or leaders. Also, this approach precludes reaching a priori conclusions about two other important empirical questions raised by Merton, whether any phenomenon is ever functional or dysfunctional for an entire society, and if functional, whether it is therefore indispensable to that society.[9]

In a modern heterogeneous society, few phenomena are functional or dysfunctional for the society as a whole and most result in benefits to some groups and costs to others.

Given the level of differentiation in modern society, I am even skeptical that one can empirically identify a social system called society. Society exists, of course, but it is closer to being a very large aggregate, and when sociologists talk about society as a system, they often really mean the nation.

I would also argue that no social phenomenon is indispensable; it may be too powerful or too highly valued to be eliminated, but in most instances, one can suggest what Merton calls "functional alternatives" or equivalents for social phenomena, that is, other social patterns or policies that achieve the same functions but avoid the dysfunctions.

THE FUNCTIONS OF POVERTY

The conventional view of American poverty is so dedicated to identifying the dysfunctions of poverty, for both the poor and the nation, that at first glance it seems inconceivable that poverty could be functional for anyone. Of course, the slumlord and the loan shark are widely known to profit from the existence of poverty, but they are popularly viewed as evil men and their activities are, at least in part, dysfunctional for the poor. What is less often recognized, at least in the conventional wisdom, is that poverty also makes possible the existence or expansion of "respectable" professions and occupations, for example, penology, criminology, social work, and public health. More recently, the poor have provided jobs for professional and paraprofessional "poverty warriors," as well as for journalists and social scientists, this author included, who have supplied the information demanded since public curiosity about the poor developed in the 1960s.

Clearly, then, poverty and the poor serve a number of

functions for affluent groups—households, professions, institutions, corporations, and classes, among others—thus
contributing to the persistence of these groups, which in
turn encourages the persistence of poverty in dialectical
fashion. These functions are not, however, necessarily the
causes of poverty, for functions are, by definition, effects
and not causes, and my analysis is more concerned with
showing how the functions of poverty aid in the persistence
of nonpoor groups than with determining the causes of
the persistence of poverty. I shall describe fifteen sets of
such functions—economic, social, cultural, and political—
that seem to me most significant.

First, the existence of poverty makes sure that "dirty"
work is done. Every economy has such work: physically
dirty or dangerous, temporary, dead-end and underpaid,
undignified and menial jobs. In America, poverty functions
to provide a low-wage labor pool that is willing—or rather,
unable to be unwilling—to perform dirty work at low
cost.[10] Indeed, this function is so important that in some
Southern states, welfare payments have been cut off during
the summer months when the poor are needed to work in
the fields. Furthermore, many economic activities involving dirty work depend heavily on the poor; restaurants,
hospitals, parts of the garment industry, and industrial
agriculture, among others, could not persist in their present
form without their dependence on the substandard wages
they pay their employees.

Second, the poor subsidize, directly and indirectly,
many activities that benefit affluent people and institutions.[11] For one thing, they have long supported both the
consumption and the investment activities of the private
economy by virtue of the low wages they receive. This was
openly advocated at the beginning of the Industrial Revolution, when a French writer quoted by T. H. Marshall

pointed out that "to assure and maintain the prosperities of our industries, it is necessary that the workers should never acquire wealth."[12] Examples of this kind of subsidization abound even today; for example, poorly paid domestics subsidize the upper middle and upper classes, making life easier for their employers and freeing affluent women for a variety of professional, cultural, civic, or social activities. Conversely, because the rich do not have to subsidize the poor, they can divert a higher proportion of their income to savings and investment and thus fuel economic growth. This in turn can produce higher incomes for everybody, including the poor, although it does not necessarily improve the position of the poor in the socioeconomic hierarchy, since the benefits of economic growth are also distributed unequally.

At the same time, the poor subsidize the governmental economy, because many of them pay a higher percentage of their income in taxes than the rest of the population. Although about a third to a half of the poor get welfare benefits and other transfer payments exceeding what they pay in taxes, those who do not get them are thus subsidizing the many state and local governmental programs that serve more affluent taxpayers.[13] The poor who do not get welfare payments also subsidize federal governmental activities, at least in the sense that they help to provide the taxes that are not paid by the rich who receive tax preferences, such as the reduced tax rate for capital gains.[14] In addition, the poor support medical innovation as patients in teaching and research hospitals and as guinea pigs in medical experiments, reducing the risk for the more affluent patients who alone can afford these innovations once they are incorporated into medical practice.

Third, poverty creates jobs for a number of occupations and professions that serve the poor, or shield the rest of the population from them. As already noted, penology would be minuscule without the poor, as would the police, since the poor provide the majority of their "clients." Other activities that flourish because of the existence of poverty are the numbers game, the sale of heroin and cheap wines and liquors, Pentecostal ministers, faith healers, prostitutes, pawnshops, and the peacetime army, which recruits its enlisted men mainly from among the poor.

Fourth, the poor buy goods that others do not want and thus prolong their economic usefulness, such as day-old bread, fruit, and vegetables that would otherwise have to be thrown out, secondhand clothes, and deteriorating automobiles and buildings. They also provide incomes for doctors, lawyers, teachers, and others who are too old, poorly trained, or incompetent to attract more affluent clients.

In addition, the poor perform a number of social and cultural functions:

Fifth, the poor can be identified and punished as alleged or real deviants in order to uphold the legitimacy of dominant norms.[15] The defenders of the desirability of hard work, thrift, honesty, and monogamy need people who can be accused of being lazy, spendthrift, dishonest, and promiscuous to justify these norms, and as Erikson and others following Durkheim have pointed out, the norms themselves are best legitimated by discovering violations.[16]

Whether the poor actually violate these norms more than affluent people is still open to question. The working poor work harder and longer than high-status jobholders, and poor housewives must do more housework to keep their slum apartments clean than their middle-class peers in standard housing. The proportion of cheaters among welfare recipients is considerably lower than among income-tax payers.[17] Violent crime is higher among the poor, but the affluent commit a variety of white-collar crimes, and several studies of self-reported delinquency have concluded that middle-class youngsters can be as delinquent as poor ones. However, the poor are more likely to be caught when participating in deviant acts, and once caught, more likely to be punished than middle-class transgressors. Moreover, they lack the political and cultural power to correct the stereotypes that affluent people hold of them and thus continue to be thought of as lazy, spendthrift, and so on, whatever the empirical evidence, by those who need living proof that deviance does not pay.[18] The actually or allegedly deviant poor have traditionally been described as undeserving, and in more recent terminology, as culturally deprived or pathological.

Sixth, another group of poor, described as deserving because they are disabled or suffering from bad luck, provide the rest of the population with different emotional satisfactions; they evoke compassion, pity, and charity, thus allowing those who help them to feel that they are altruistic, moral, and practicing the Judeo-Christian ethic. The deserving poor also enable others to feel fortunate for being spared the deprivations that come with poverty.[19]

Seventh, as a converse of the fifth function described previously, the poor offer affluent people vicarious participation in the uninhibited sexual, alcoholic, and narcotic behavior in which many poor people are alleged to indulge, and which, being freed from the constraints of affluence and respectability, they are often thought to enjoy more than the middle classes. One of the popular beliefs about welfare recipients is that they are on a continuous sex-filled vacation. Although it may be true that the poor are more given to uninhibited behavior, studies by Lee Rainwater and other observers of the lower class indicate that such behavior is as often motivated by despair as by lack of inhibition, and that it results less in pleasure than in a compulsive escape from grim reality.[20] Whether the poor actually have more sex and enjoy it more than affluent people is irrelevant; as long as the latter believe it to be so, they can share in it vicariously and perhaps enviously when instances are reported in fictional and journalistic or sociological and anthropological formats.

Eighth, poverty helps to guarantee the status of those who are not poor. In a stratified society, where social mobility is an especially important goal and class boundaries are fuzzy, people need quite urgently to know where they stand. As a result, the poor function as a reliable and relatively permanent measuring rod for status comparison, particularly for the working class, which must find and maintain status distinctions between itself and the poor, much as the aristocracy must find ways of distinguishing itself from the *nouveaux riches.*

Ninth, the poor also assist in the upward mobility of the nonpoor, for as William J. Goode has pointed out, "the privileged . . . try systematically to prevent the talent of the less privileged from being recognized or developed."[21] By being denied educational opportunities or being stereotyped as stupid or unteachable, the poor thus enable others to obtain the better jobs. Also, an unknown number of people have moved themselves or their children up in the socio-economic hierarchy through the incomes earned from the provision of goods and services to the poor, as by becoming policemen and teachers, owning "Mom and Pop" stores, or working in the various rackets that flourish in the slums.

In fact, members of almost every immigrant group have financed their upward mobility by providing retail goods and services, housing, entertainment, gambling, and narcotics to later arrivals in America (or in the city), most recently to blacks, Mexicans, and Puerto Ricans. Other Americans, of both European and native origin, have financed their entry into the upper middle and upper classes by owning or managing the illegal institutions that serve the poor, as well as the legal but not respectable ones, such as slum housing.

Tenth, just as the poor contribute to the economic viability of a number of businesses and professions (see function 3 above), they also add to the social viability of noneconomic groups. For one thing, they help to keep the aristocracy busy, thereby justifying its continued existence. "Society" uses the poor as clients of settlement houses and charity benefits, so as to practice its public-mindedness and thus demonstrate its superiority over the *nouveaux riches* who devote themselves to conspicuous consumption. The poor play a similar function for philanthropic enterprises at other levels of the socio-economic hierarchy, including the mass of middle-class civic organizations and women's clubs engaged in volunteer work and fund-raising in almost every American community. Doing good among the poor has traditionally helped the church to find a method of expressing religious sentiments in action; in recent years, militant church activity among and for the poor has enabled the church to hold on to its more liberal and radical members who might otherwise have dropped out of organized religion altogether.

Eleventh, the poor perform several cultural functions. They have played an unsung role in the creation of "civilization," having supplied the construction labor for many of the monuments often identified as the noblest expressions and examples of civilization, for example, the Egyptian pyramids, Greek temples, and medieval churches.[22] Moreover, they have helped to create a goodly share of the surplus capital that funds the artists and intellectuals who make culture, and particularly "high" culture, possible in the first place.

Twelfth, the "low" culture created for or by the poor is often adopted by the more affluent. The rich collect artifacts from extinct folk cultures (though not only from poor ones), and almost all Americans listen to the jazz, blues, spirituals, and country music which originated among the Southern poor—as well as rock, which was derived from similar sources. The protest of the poor sometimes becomes literature; in 1970, for example, poetry written by ghetto children became popular in sophisticated literary circles. The poor also serve as culture heroes and literary subjects, particularly of course for the Left, though the hobo, cowboy, hipster, and mythical prostitute with a heart of gold have performed this function for a variety of groups.

Finally, the poor carry out a number of important political functions:

Thirteenth, the poor serve as symbolic constituencies and opponents for several political groups. For example, parts of the revolutionary left could not exist without the poor, particularly now that the working class can no longer be perceived as the vanguard of the revolution. Conversely, political groups of conservative bent use the "welfare chiselers" and others who "live off the taxpayer's hard-earned money" to justify their demands for reductions in welfare payments and tax relief. Moreover, the role of the poor in upholding dominant norms (see function 5 above) also has a significant political function. An economy based on the ideology of laissez-faire requires a deprived population that is supposedly unwilling to work; not only does the alleged moral inferiority of the poor reduce the moral pressure on the present political economy to eliminate poverty, but redistributive alternatives can be made to look quite unattractive if those who will benefit from them most can be described as lazy, spendthrift, dishonest, and promiscuous. Thus, conservatives and classic liberals would find it difficult to justify some of their political beliefs without the poor—but then, so would modern liberals and socialists who seek to eliminate poverty.

Fourteenth, the poor, being powerless, can be made to absorb the economic and political costs of change and growth in American society. During the nineteenth century, they did the backbreaking work that built the cities; today, they are pushed out of their neighborhoods to make room for "progress." Urban renewal projects to hold middle-class taxpayers and stores in the city and expressways to enable suburbanites to commute downtown have typically been located in poor neighborhoods, since no other group will allow itself to be displaced. For much the same reason, urban universities, hospitals, and civic centers also expand into land occupied by the poor. The major costs of the industrialization of agriculture in America have been borne by the poor, who are pushed off the land without recompense, just as in earlier centuries in Europe they bore the brunt of the transformation of agrarian societies into industrial ones. The poor have also paid a large share of the human cost of the growth of American power overseas, for they have provided many of the foot soldiers for Vietnam and other wars.

Fifteenth, the poor have played an important role in shaping the American political process; because they vote and participate less than other groups, the political system has often been free to ignore them. This has not only made American politics more centrist than would otherwise be the case, but it has also added to the stability of the political process for the rest of the population. If the 12 percent of Americans below the federal poverty line participated fully in the political process, they would almost certainly demand better jobs and higher incomes, which would require some income redistribution and would thus generate further political conflict between the haves and the have-nots. Moreover, when the poor do participate, they often provide the Democrats with a captive constituency, for they can rarely support Republicans, lack parties of their own, and thus have no other place to go politically. This in turn has enabled the Democrats to count on their votes, allowing the party to be more responsive to voters who might otherwise switch to the Republicans.

Functional Alternatives for Poverty

I have described fifteen of the more important functions that the poor carry out in American society, enough to support the functionalist thesis that poverty survives in part because it is useful to a number of groups in society. This analysis is not intended to suggest that because it is functional, poverty *should* persist, or that it *must* persist. Whether or not it should persist is a normative question; whether it must, an analytic and empirical one; but the answer to both depends in part on whether the dysfunctions of poverty outweigh the functions. Obviously, poverty has many dysfunctions, mainly for the poor themselves, but also for the more affluent. For example, the social order of the affluent is upset by the pathology, crime, political protest, and disruption emanating from the poor, and their income is affected by the taxes that must be levied to protect their social order. Whether or not the dysfunctions outweigh the functions is a question that clearly deserves more study.

It is, however, possible to suggest alternatives for

many of the functions of the poor. Thus, society's dirty work (function 1) could be done without poverty, some by automating it, the rest by paying the workers who do it decent wages, which would help considerably to cleanse that kind of work. Nor is it necessary for the poor to subsidize the activities they support through their low-wage jobs (function 2), for like dirty work, many of these activities are essential enough to persist even if wages were raised. In both instances, however, costs would be driven up, resulting in higher prices to the customers and clients of dirty work and subsidized activity, with obvious dysfunctional consequences for more affluent people.

Alternative roles for the professionals who flourish because of the poor (function 3) are easy to suggest. Social workers could counsel the affluent, as most prefer to do anyway, and the police could devote themselves to traffic and organized crime. Fewer penologists would be employable, however, and Pentecostal religion would probably not survive without the poor. Nor would parts of the secondhand and thirdhand market (function 4), although even affluent people sometimes buy used goods. Other roles would have to be found for badly trained or incompetent professionals now relegated to serving the poor, and someone else would have to pay their salaries.

Alternatives for the deviance-connected social functions (functions 5–7) can be found more easily and cheaply than for the economic functions. Other groups are already available to serve as deviants to uphold traditional morality—entertainers, hippies, and most recently, adolescents in general. These same groups are also available as alleged or real orgiasts to provide vicarious participation in sexual fantasies. The disabled already function as objects of pity and charity, and the poor may therefore not even be needed for functions 5–7.

The status and mobility functions of the poor (functions 8 and 9) are far more difficult to replace. In a hierarchical society, some people must be defined as inferior to everyone else with respect to a variety of attributes, and the poor perform this function more adequately than others. They could, however, perform it without being as poverty-stricken as they are, and one can conceive of a stratification system in which the people below the federal poverty line would receive 60 percent of the median income rather than 40 percent or less, as is now the case—even though they would still be last in the pecking order.[23] Needless to say, such a reduction of economic inequality would also require income redistribution. Given the opposition to income redistribution among more affluent people, however, it seems unlikely that the status functions of poverty can be eliminated, and these—together with the economic functions of the poor, which are equally expensive to replace—may turn out to be the major obstacles to the elimination of poverty.

The role of the poor in the upward mobility of other groups could be maintained without their being so low in income. However, if their incomes were raised above subsistence levels, they would begin to generate capital so that their own entrepreneurs could supply them with goods and services, thus competing with and perhaps rejecting "outside" suppliers. Indeed, this is already happening in a number of ghettos, where blacks are replacing white storeowners.

Similarly, if the poor were more affluent, they would make less willing clients for upper-class and middle-class philanthropic and religious groups (function 10), though as long as they are economically and otherwise unequal, this function need not disappear altogether. Moreover, some would still use the settlement houses and other philanthropic institutions to pursue individual upward mobility, as they do now.

The cultural functions (11 and 12) may not need to be replaced. In America, the labor unions have rarely allowed the poor to help build cultural monuments anyway, and there is sufficient surplus capital from other sources to subsidize the unprofitable components of high culture. Similarly, other deviant groups are available to innovate in popular culture and supply new culture heroes.

Some of the political functions of the poor would be as difficult to replace as their economic and status functions. Although the poor could probably continue to serve as symbolic constituencies and opponents (function 13) if their incomes were raised while they remained unequal in other respects, increases in income are generally accompanied by increases in power as well. Consequently, once they were no longer so poor, people would be likely to resist paying the costs of growth and change (function 14), and it would be difficult to find alternative groups who could be displaced for urban renewal and technological "progress." Of course, it is possible to design city rebuilding and highway projects that properly reimburse the displaced people, but such projects would then become considerably more expensive, thus raising the price for those now benefitting from urban renewal and expressways. Alternatively, many might never be built, thus reducing the comfort and convenience of those beneficiaries. Similarly, if the poor were subjected to less economic pressure, they would probably be less willing to serve in the army, except at considerably higher pay, in which case war would become yet more costly and thus less popular politically. Alternatively, more servicemen would have to be recruited from the middle and upper classes, but this also would make war less popular.

The political stabilizing and "centering" role of the poor (function 15) probably cannot be substituted for at all, since no other group is willing to be disenfranchised or likely enough to remain apathetic so as to reduce the fragility of the political system. Moreover, if the poor were given higher incomes, they would probably become more active politically, thus adding their demands to those of other groups already putting pressure on the political allocators of resources. They might remain loyal to the Democratic party, but like other moderate-income voters, they might also be attracted to the Republicans or to third parties. While improving the economic status of the currently poor would not necessarily drive the political system far to the left, it would enlarge the constituencies now demanding higher wages and more public funds. The currently poor could also be replaced by new poor immigrants from Europe and elsewhere, who could serve as non-participating "ballast" in the polity, at least until they became sufficiently Americanized to demand a participatory role.

In sum, then, several of the most important functions of the poor cannot be replaced with alternatives, while some could be replaced but almost always only at higher costs to other people, particularly more affluent ones. Consequently, *a functional analysis must conclude that poverty persists not only because it satisfies a number of functions but also because many of the functional alternatives to poverty would be quite dysfunctional for the more affluent members of society.*[24]

RADICAL FUNCTIONAL ANALYSIS

I noted earlier that functional analysis had itself become a maligned phenomenon and that a secondary purpose of this chapter was to demonstrate its continued usefulness. One reason for its present low status is political; insofar as an analysis of functions, particularly latent functions, seems to justify what ought to be condemned, it appears to lend itself to the support of conservative ideological positions, although it can also have radical implications when it subverts the conventional wisdom. Still, as Merton has pointed out, functional analysis per se is ideologically neutral,[25] and "like other forms of sociological analysis, it can be infused with any of a wide range of sociological values."[26] This infusion depends, of course, on the purposes—and even the functions—of the functional analysis, for as Louis Wirth suggested long ago, "every assertion of a 'fact' about the social world touches the interests of some individual or group,"[27] and even if functional analyses are conceived and conducted in a neutral manner, they are rarely interpreted in an ideological vacuum.

In one sense, my analysis is neutral: if one makes no judgment as to whether poverty ought to be eliminated—and if one can subsequently avoid being accused of acquiescing in poverty—then the analysis suggests only that poverty persists because it is useful to many groups in society.[28] If one favors the elimination of poverty, however, then the analysis can have a variety of political implications, *depending in part on how completely it is carried out.*

If functional analysis only identifies the functions of social phenomena without mentioning their dysfunctions, then it may, intentionally or otherwise, agree with or support holders of conservative values. Thus, to say only that the poor perform many functions for the rich might be interpreted or used to justify poverty, just as Davis and Moore's argument that social stratification is functional because it provides society with highly trained professionals could be taken to justify inequality.[29]

Actually, the Davis and Moore analysis was conservative because it was incomplete; it did not identify the dysfunctions of inequality and failed to suggest functional alternatives, as Tumin and Schwartz have pointed out.[30] Once a functional analysis is made more nearly complete by the addition of functional alternatives, it can take on a liberal reform cast, because the alternatives often provide ameliorative policies that do not require any drastic change in the existing social order, although radical functional alternatives are also possible.

Even so, to make functional analysis complete requires yet another step, an examination of the functional alternatives themselves. My analysis suggests that the alternatives for poverty are themselves dysfunctional for the affluent population, and it ultimately comes to a conclusion not very different from that of radical sociologists. To wit: *that social phenomena which are functional for affluent groups and dysfunctional for poor ones persist; that if the elimination of such phenomena through functional alternatives generates dysfunctions for the affluent, these phenomena will continue to persist; and that phenomena like poverty can be eliminated only when they either become sufficiently dysfunctional for the affluent (for example, by high crime rates making their lives miserable even in the suburbs), or when the poor can obtain enough power to change the system of social stratification.*[31]

The Functions of Inequality

The observations about the functions of poverty also apply to inequality; it too has positive functions for many individuals and groups, which must be replaced by functional alternatives if inequality is to be reduced. Moreover, such functional alternatives would hurt the groups that now benefit from inequality, and they can only come into being when the dysfunctions of inequality become so great as to motivate its beneficiaries to reduce it, or when the victims of inequality can obtain power—either to reduce it or to shift it to another group in society.

The functions of inequality are, however, much harder to identify than those of poverty, for inequality is more pervasive than poverty, and it exists in many different ways and at different levels of the socio-economic hierarchy. Thus, inequality between the upper and upper middle classes has different functions than that between the upper and lower classes, or that between parents and their children. Consequently, a functional analysis of the myriad kinds of inequality would require a book of its own, and this chapter can only serve as a model for such an analysis.

Like poverty, inequality has economic, social, cultural, and political functions. Its most important economic functions are to maintain the existing division of labor and to sort people into the existing roles, filling roles for which the supply of labor exceeds the demand by justifying lower wages, and filling those where the supply is insufficient to meet the demand by paying higher ones. At the same time, inequality functions to block access to the most rewarded roles by setting up various obstacles to people's competing for them. For example, it would be inconceivable for a poor man to run for president. In addition, inequality provides a method of rationing scarce resources, frequently by giving them to those who already have them.

Inequality also creates work for a number of occupations that enable people either to cope with inequality and some of its more deleterious consequences. For example, various secular and sacred forms of therapy serve patients who have been hurt by inequality, and religion exists in part because it provides a respected moral code—or another world—in which equality or justice and fairness prevail.

Inequality is of course tautologous with the class hierarchy, but insofar as upward mobility satisfies ego needs for striving and self-fulfillment, providing people with easily visible goals toward which to aspire, it is perhaps the most important noneconomic function of inequality. As for cultural functions, inequality not only helps to create cultural diversity, because differences of income and education result in differences of taste, but it also provides raw material for culture itself, for a great deal of both serious and popular fiction—in the printed, electronic, and visual media—is concerned with coming to grips with inequality, describing its workings, and healing its wounds. Finally, inequality has important political functions, for insofar as politics has to do with the allocation of scarce resources, it could not exist without inequality. In a completely egalitarian society, there would be less need for politicians to determine who gets what, since most resources would be allocated on egalitarian principles.

This brief set of observations cannot do justice to the functions of inequality. For one thing, it has focused only on inequalities of income and power. A more comprehensive analysis would have to deal with the functions of age inequality, which maintains the existence of schools and all other child-rearing agencies that enable young people to become adults but also make sure that the primacy of adult authority and knowledge is upheld; and with the functions of racial, sexual, and all other kinds of inequality.

Whether functional alternatives for inequality can be developed is an open question; indeed, answering this question is a major task for egalitarian policy. Like those of poverty, the various psychological and cultural functions of inequality can perhaps be replaced or at least diverted to less harmful forms, for example, by replacing money and power as goals of upward mobility with competition for excellence in leisure. The economic, social, and political functions of inequality are much harder to substitute for, again because their replacement would be dysfunctional for those who benefit from it. Nor is it realistic to imagine that inequality would ever become so dysfunctional that its beneficiaries would act to abolish it, although it is more realistic to imagine that the unequal would try to obtain political power to reduce it. The poor are too small a minority to have much hope of drastically increasing their power, even by revolutionary means, but the less-than-equal are a much larger proportion of the population however inequality is measured, and if the trends I describe in Part I accelerate, it is possible that functional alternatives for some kinds of inequality will have to be found.

NOTES

This is a slightly revised version of "The Positive Functions of Poverty," published in the *American Journal of Sociology*, vol. 78 (September 1972), pp. 275–89. The final section was written especially for this volume. The original paper was prepared for a project on stratification and poverty of the American Academy of Arts and Sciences, under a grant from the Ford Foundation.

1. Robert K. Merton, "Manifest and Latent Functions," in his *Social Theory and Social Structure* (Glencoe, Ill.: Free Press, 1949), pp. 21–82, quote at p. 49, and in subsequent editions.
2. This essay also has the latent function, as S. M. Miller has suggested, of contributing to the long debate over the functional analysis of social stratification presented by Kingsley Davis and Wilbert Moore, "Some Principles of Stratification," *American Sociological Review*, vol. 10 (April 1945), pp. 242–9.
3. Merton, "Manifest and Latent Functions," p. 50.
4. *Ibid.*, p. 51.
5. *Ibid.*
6. Probably one of the few instances in which a phenomenon has the same function for two groups with different interests is when

the survival of the system in which both participate is at stake. Thus, a wage increase can be functional for labor and dysfunctional for management (and consumers), but if the wage increase endangers the firm's survival, it is dysfunctional for labor as well. This assumes, however, that the firm's survival is valued by the workers, which may not always be the case, for example when jobs are available elsewhere.

7. In his 1949 article, Merton described functions and dysfunctions in terms of encouraging or hindering adaptation or adjustment to a system, although subsequently he has written that "dysfunction refers to the particular inadequacies of a particular part of the system for a designated requirement" ("Social Problems and Sociological Theory," in Robert K. Merton and Robert Nisbet, eds., *Contemporary Social Problems* [New York: Harcourt, Brace & Co., 1961], p. 732). Since adaptation and adjustment to a system can have conservative ideological implications, Merton's later formulation and my own definitional approach make it easier to use functional analysis as an ideologically neutral or at least ideologically variable method, insofar as the researcher can decide whether he or she supports the values of the group under analysis.

8. It should be noted, however, that there are no absolute benefits and costs, just as there are no absolute functions and dysfunctions; not only are one group's benefits often another group's costs, but every group defines benefits by its own manifest and latent values, and a social scientist or planner who has determined that certain phenomena provide beneficial consequences for a group may find that the group thinks otherwise. For example, during the 1960s, advocates of racial integration discovered that a significant portion of the black community no longer considered it a benefit but saw it rather as a policy to assimilate blacks into white society and to decimate the political power of the black community.

9. Merton, "Manifest and Latent Functions," pp. 32–6.

10. On the economic functions of the poor and of welfare, see Frances F. Piven and Richard A. Cloward, *Regulating the Poor* (New York: Pantheon Books, 1971).

11. Of course, the poor do not actually subsidize the affluent. Rather, by being forced to work for low wages, they enable the affluent to use the money saved in this fashion for other purposes. The concept of subsidy used here thus assumes belief in a "just wage."

12. T. H. Marshall, "Poverty and Inequality," unpublished paper

prepared for a project on stratification and poverty of the American Academy of Arts and Sciences, n.d., p. 7.

13. Joseph A. Pechman, "The Rich, the Poor, and the Taxes They Pay," *The Public Interest*, no. 17 (Fall 1969), pp. 21–44, especially p. 33.

14. For an estimate of how these tax preferences affect different income groups, see Joseph A. Pechman, and Benjamin A. Okner, "Individual Tax Erosion by Income Classes," paper prepared for the United States Joint Economic Committee, January 14, 1972.

15. David Macarov, *Incentives to Work* (San Francisco: Jossey-Bass, Publishers, 1970), pp. 31–3. See also Lee Rainwater, "Neutralizing the Disinherited," in Vernon Allen, ed., *Psychological Factors in Poverty* (Chicago: Markham Pub. Co., 1970), pp. 9–28.

16. Kai T. Erikson, "Notes on the Sociology of Deviance," in Howard S. Becker, ed., *The Other Side: Perspectives on Deviance* (New York: Free Press, 1964), pp. 9–22.

17. Most official investigations of welfare cheating have concluded that less than 5 percent of recipients are on the rolls illegally, while it has been estimated that about a third of the population cheats in filing income tax returns.

18. Although this chapter deals with the functions of poverty for other groups, poverty has often been described as a motivating or character-building device for the poor themselves, and economic conservatives have argued that by generating the incentive to work, poverty encourages the poor to escape poverty.

19. A psychiatrist has even proposed the fantastic hypothesis that the rich and the poor are engaged in a sadomasochistic relationship, the latter being supported financially by the former so that they can gratify their sadistic needs. Joseph Chernus, "Cities: A Study in Sadomasochism," *Medical Opinion and Review*, May 1967, pp. 104–9.

20. Lee Rainwater, *Behind Ghetto Walls* (Chicago: Aldine Publishing Co., 1970).

21. William J. Goode, "The Protection of the Inept," *American Sociological Review*, vol. 32 (February 1967), pp. 5–19, quotation at p. 5.

22. Although this is not a contemporary function of poverty in America, it should be noted that today these monuments serve to attract and gratify American tourists.

23. Of course, most of the poor earn less than 40 percent of the median, and about a third of them, less than 20 percent of the median.

24. Or as Bruno Stein puts it: "If the non-poor make the rules . . . antipoverty efforts will only be made up to the point where the needs of the non-poor are satisfied, rather than the needs of the poor." *On Relief* (New York: Basic Books, 1971), p. 171.

25. Merton, "Manifest and Latent Functions," p. 43, and "Social Problems and Sociological Theory," pp. 736–7.

26. Merton, "Manifest and Latent Functions," p. 40.

27. Louis Wirth, Preface to Karl Mannheim, *Ideology and Utopia* (New York: Harcourt, Brace & Co., 1936), p. xvii.

28. Even in this case the analysis need not be purely neutral, but can be put to important policy uses, for example by indicating more effectively than moral attacks on poverty the exact nature of the obstacles that must be overcome if poverty is to be eliminated. See also Merton, "Social Problems and Sociological Theory," pp. 709–12.

29. Davis and Moore, "Some Principles of Stratification."

30. Melvin M. Tumin, "Some Principles of Stratification: A Critical Analysis," *American Sociological Review*, vol. 18 (August 1953), pp. 387–93; Richard D. Schwartz, "Functional Alternatives to Inequality," *American Sociological Review*, vol. 20 (August 1955), pp. 424–30. Functional analysis can of course be conservative in value or have conservative implications for a number of other reasons, principally in its overt or covert comparison of the advantages of functions and disadvantages of dysfunctions, or in its attitudes toward the groups that are benefitting and paying the costs. Thus, a conservatively inclined policy researcher could conclude that the dysfunctions of poverty far outnumber the functions, but still decide that the needs of the poor are simply not as important or worthy as those of other groups, or of the country as a whole.

31. On the possibilities of radical functional analysis, see Merton, "Manifest and Latent Functions," pp. 40–3, and Alvin Gouldner, *The Coming Crisis of Western Sociology* (New York: Basic Books, 1970), p. 443. One difference between my analysis and the prevailing radical view is that most of the functions I have described are latent, whereas many radicals treat them as manifest: recognized and intended by an unjust economic system to oppress the poor. Practically speaking, however, this difference may be unimportant, for if unintended and unrecognized functions were recognized, many affluent people might then decide that they ought to be intended as well, so as to forestall a more expensive antipoverty effort that might be dysfunctional for them.

5
Political Inequality and Majority Rule

Many of America's troubles are located in the city and have therefore often been treated as urban. The real crisis is not urban, however, but national, and it stems in considerable part from the political inequality that is built into American democracy. Much of that inequality can in turn be traced to economic inequality, but even the formal structures of American democracy contribute to political inequality, and this chapter focuses on those particularly affecting the poor and the black, notably the dependence of the polity on majority rule.

THE NATIONAL PROBLEMS OF THE CITY

The city's troubles have been catalogued in long and by now familiar lists, but they boil down to three basic ones:

poverty and segregation, with all their consequences for both their direct victims and other urban residents; and economic decline, the decreasing role of the city in the national economy, with all its consequences for the ability of the city to provide jobs and services and levy taxes. Moreover, the first two problems are actually a partial cause of the third, for the costs of helping the poor and isolating them from the rest of the population and the inability of the poor to pay their share of keeping up the city have contributed to its financial straits. In addition, the increasing proportion of poor and black people in city populations has accelerated the exodus of the middle class and those parts of the urban economy that cater to it, and have discouraged the development of new urban industries. Consequently, the elimination of urban poverty and segregation would not only relieve the misery of their victims, but would encourage and enable them to improve the urban condition, even if they could not restore the city to its once central position in the national economy.

Neither poverty and segregation nor economic decline is unique to the city, and more important, all three are caused by nation-wide conditions. Poverty is to a considerable extent a by-product of the American economy, which has been able to create affluence and near-affluence for about two-thirds of the country only by excluding the remaining third and forcing them to live in poverty or near-poverty. Moreover, economic growth today is concentrated in the industries and services that employ the skilled, semi-professional, and professional worker, and in fact, many of the unskilled now living in urban slums were driven out of rural areas where the demand for their labor had dried up even earlier than in the cities. Segregation has always been part and parcel of the national social structure, while economic decline is exacerbated by nation-wide technological changes and suburbanization, both of which affect not only the cities but all older communities.

THE AMERICAN FAILURE

The failure of America to deal with the twin evils of poverty and segregation has often been ascribed to a lack of national will, as if the country were an individual who could pull himself or herself together if he or she only wanted to; but even the miraculous emergence of a national consensus would be insufficient, for the sources of America's failure are built into its most important economic and political institutions.

One major source of failure is to be found in the corporate economy, which has not dealt with or been made to deal with the fact that the rural and urban unskilled workers it has cast aside are part of the same economic process that has created affluence or near-affluence for the majority of Americans. Private enterprise has been able to improve productivity and profit without having to charge against its profit the third of the total population in poverty or near-poverty. Instead, government has been left with the responsibility for this by-product of the economic process, just as it has often been given the task of removing the waste materials and pollutants that are by-products of the production process.

But government has not been able or willing to require private enterprise—and its own public agencies—to incorporate the employable poor into the economy. Not only is there as yet little recognition among the general public or most of our leaders of the extent to which urban and rural poverty result from the structure of the economy, but private enterprise is powerful enough to persuade most

people that government should take care of the poor, or
subsidize industry to create jobs for them.

However, governments, federal, state, and local, have
not been able or willing to absorb responsibility for the
poor either, and for several important political reasons.
First, most voters—and the politicians that represent them
—are not inclined to give the cities the funds and powers
to deal with poverty or segregation. This disinclination is
by no means as arbitrary as it may seem, for the plight of
the urban poor, the anger of the militant blacks, and the
economic difficulties of the city have not yet hurt or even
seriously inconvenienced the rest of the country. Rural
and small-town America make little use of the city anyway,
except for occasional tourist forays, and the urban corporations and financial institutions that play an influential part
in city economies are not impaired in their functioning by
the urban condition. Suburbanites may complain about the
dirt, crime, and traffic congestion when they commute to
city jobs, but they can still get downtown without difficulty, and besides, many of their employers are also
moving out to the suburbs. In addition, the suburbs have
more than enough power to keep urban problems, not to
mention the urban poor and black, out of their bailiwicks
through zoning and other devices. But even the city
dwellers who are neither poor nor black can pursue their
daily routines unchanged, for most of them never need
to enter the slum areas and ghettos. Only the urbanites who
work in these areas or live near them are directly touched
by the urban condition—but they are a small minority of
America's voters. To be sure, the fear of crime now grips
many Americans wherever they live, but most people have
not yet become aware of the causal connection between
crime and poverty or still hope that more police protection
will reduce crime.

Second, many Americans, regardless of where they live, are opposed to significant governmental activity in behalf of the poor and black. Not only do they consider taxes an imposition on their ability to spend their earnings, but they view governmental expenditure as economic waste. The average American taxpayer is generous in paying for the defense of the country and for wars that increase American power and prestige in the world, but is often opposed to governmental activities that help anyone other than himself. The very corporations and workers whose incomes depend on government contracts oppose federal support of other activities and groups—and without ever becoming aware of the contradiction.

Consequently, many taxpayers and voters refuse to see the extent to which governmental activities create jobs and provide incomes, and how much government subsidizes some sectors of American life but not others. These subsidies go mainly to the affluent, and the only significant grant to the poor is public welfare. But it is considered a handout, not a subsidy.

In addition, subsidies are generally allocated on the basis of power, not need, and this is a third reason for the lack of action in the cities. Even though many Americans live in the city, urban areas and their political representatives have little power, and the poor of course still less. The poor are powerless because they are a minority of the population, are not organized politically, are often difficult to organize, and are not even a homogeneous group with similar interests that could be organized into a single pressure group. The cities are relatively powerless because of the gerrymandering of American state governments in favor of rural and small-town areas. As a result, rural-dominated state legislatures can use the tax receipts of the cities to subsidize their own areas, and legislators from these areas have been able to outvote the representatives of urban constituencies. The Supreme Court's requirement of "one person, one vote" is now bringing about reapportionment, but it is too late to help the cities. As more and more Americans leave for the suburbs, the cities will not be able to increase their power, for voters and politicians from rural and suburban areas who share a common interest in not helping the cities can unite against them.

In effect, then, the cities and the poor and the black are politically outnumbered. This state of affairs suggests the fourth and perhaps most important reason for the national failure to act: the structure of American democracy and particularly the consequences of majority rule.

THE POLITICS OF MAJORITY RULE

America, more so than other democratic nations in the world, runs its polity on the basis of majority rule. A majority vote in its various political institutions determines who will be nominated and elected to office, what legislation will be passed and funded, and who will be appointed to run the administering agencies. Of course, the candidates, laws, and budgets that are subject to the vote of the majority are almost always determined by minorities; the only persons who can run for office these days are either affluent or financed by the affluent groups who donate the campaign funds, and the legislation they vote on is often suggested or even drafted by campaign-fund donors or other small groups with specific interests in government action. Properly speaking, then, American democracy allows affluent minorities to propose and the majority to dispose.

Elitist or conspiratorial theories are not necessary to

explain this phenomenon, for it follows from the nature of American political participation, and from the nature of politics itself. Although every citizen is urged to be active in the affairs of the community and the nation, in actual practice these rules mean that political participation is carried out by two kinds of groups, fairly permanent organized pressure groups or lobbies who want something from government, and transitory groups who are unhappy about a specific government action or inaction and may organize only to protest. (These types of participation are rare in Europe, where the opportunities for citizen participation are limited, and industrial pressure groups to obtain government contracts or real estate lobbies to prevent the construction of public housing are rare.) As a result, legislation in America tends to favor the interests of businessmen, not consumers, even though the latter are a vast majority; of landlords, not tenants; of doctors, not patients. Only organized interest groups have the specific concerns and the time, staff, and money to bring their demands before government officials. Unorganized citizens may gripe about the lack of consumer legislation or even the defense budget, but only when their interests are similar and immediately threatened so that they can organize or be organized are they able to affect government affairs.

Nevertheless, the fault lies not only with participation patterns but also with their consequences. Political decision-making is regressive; power accrues to those who already have it, and only rarely to those who need more of it. In addition, access to the decision-makers is easier for those who have had previous access and for the more powerful, and they often try to block access to competing interests and the unorganized populace. This is particularly true for issues that concern only a part of the population, and frequently small but influential interest groups can shape legislation that deprives larger numbers of people because the majority does not care about the issue and thus fails to contribute to public opinion, which, when it exists, can sway the legislators. When the majority cares deeply about an issue, government usually takes its public opinion into account, and the huge budgets for space exploration and the Vietnam war could not have been appropriated during the 1960s if the majority of the population had not been favorably inclined toward both these activities. Conversely, one reason there is no federal mass-transit program to speak of is that the majority of Americans, even in the cities, prefer to use their cars; and Congress can pay more attention to a small number of tobacco farmers and producers than to the danger of cigarette smoking because the majority of the population is not sufficiently concerned about this danger.

But while the American polity often satisfies the majority, and more important, the coalitions of minorities that make up the majority for most political issues, it also creates *outvoted minorities* who can be held down by majority rule, such as the poor and the black. Outvoted minorities are not totally without political resources, of course, but generally speaking they obtain only the leftovers from the political dinner table. For example, they can rely on the good will of the majority to do the moral thing, but this time-honored approach has so far produced only charity-level gains—accompanied by dehumanizing rules as in public welfare.

Today, many outvoted minorities have tired of waiting for an upturn in public altruism, and are exerting political pressure on the majority. Some of the poor and the black have been organizing their own pressure groups, forming coalitions with more powerful minorities—like the progressive wing of the labor movement—and obtaining support from liberals, other advocates of social justice, and guilt-ridden whites. Indeed, such methods brought about some of the civil rights and antipoverty programs of the 1960s.

Even so, these gains, however much of an improvement they represent over the past, were small even in the 1960s before they began to evaporate in the 1970s, and they did not significantly improve the living conditions of large numbers in the slums and ghettos. Moreover, the activities of ghetto demonstrators and rioters cooled much of the ardor of white liberals and trade unionists, and it is questionable whether many other groups would derive much benefit from coalition with poor or black organizations. Like most outvoted minorities, they can offer little to a coalition except the moral urgency of their cause.

Consequently, the poor and the black are caught in an almost hopeless political bind, for given the antagonism toward them on the part of many Americans, any programs that would provide them with significant gains are likely to be voted down by a majority. Legislative proposals for a massive antipoverty effort or an effective assault on segregation have always run into concerted and united opposition in Washington, because one of the few issues on which diverse and otherwise divided legislators (and their vocal constituents) can agree is to restrict and water down progressive legislation that would benefit the poor and the black. Moreover, since the poor and the black will probably always be outvoted by a majority, they are thus doomed to be *permanently outvoted minorities*. No wonder, then, that black militants demand local control; they want to opt out of a system in which they are always subject to the tyranny of the majority; or that radicals condemn democracy as a bourgeois dictatorship. Their charges are not quite as inaccurate as their exaggerated rhetoric would suggest, for what they are really saying is that in the present political system, the demands of the poor and the black will never be approved by the rest of the population.

But if I am correct in arguing that the urban condition cannot be improved until poverty and segregation are eliminated or at least sharply reduced, it is likely that *under the present structure of American politics and government, there cannot be and will not be a real solution to the problems of the cities and of the nation.*

The only other source of power left to outvoted minorities is disruption, upsetting the orderly processes of government and of daily life so as to inconvenience or threaten more powerful groups. This explains why the ghettos have rebelled, why young people sometimes resort to what adults consider meaningless delinquency, students to the occupation of school buildings, or working-class whites to occasionally violent forms of backlash.

Although disruption is bitterly attacked as antisocial by defenders of the existing social order, strikes also were once considered antisocial, though they are now so legitimate that they are no longer even thought of as a form of disruption. The disrupters of today do not strike, but their methods have not been as unproductive as their opponents would have us believe. The ghetto rebellions were responsible for temporarily stimulating private enterprise to find jobs for the so-called hard-core unemployed; the sit-ins of the welfare rights movement did win higher grants for welfare recipients in some cities, at least for a time; and the uprisings by college and high school students have been effective in winning some a voice in their schools.

Needless to say, disruption also has disadvantages: the possibility that it will be accompanied by violence and followed by counterdisruption—for example, police or vigilante violence—and by political efforts of a more powerful group to wipe out the gains achieved through disruption. Thus, the backlash generated by the ghetto rebellions has been partially responsible for the cutback in antipoverty and civil rights efforts, and the disruptions by welfare recipients and college students eventually produced repressive legislation against both groups. But disruption also creates serious costs for the rest of society, particularly through the yet greater polarization of opposing groups, the hardening of attitudes among other citizens, and the hysterical atmosphere which then results in more repressive legislation. Clearly, disruption is not the ideal way for outvoted minorities to achieve their demands, and more effective and peaceful ways of meeting them need to be found.

From Majoritarian to Egalitarian Democracy

If the outvoted minorities are to be properly represented in the political structure, two kinds of changes are necessary. First, they must be counted properly, by being persuaded or required to vote, and they must be counted fairly, without resort to gerrymandering and other ways of nullifying their vote, so that they are actually involved in the decision-making process and are not overpowered by other minorities who would be outvoted were they not affluent enough to shape the political agenda. But since even a fairer and more proper counting of the voters would still leave the outvoted minorities with little clout, ways of restricting majority rule must be found when that rule is always deaf to their demands.

Majority rule is, of course, one of the unquestioned traditions of American political life, for the first axiom of democracy has always been that the majority should decide. But democracy is not inviolably equivalent to majority rule, for government of the people, by the people, and for the people need not mean that a majority is "the people." Indeed, despite its traditional usage in democracies, majority rule is little more than an easily applied quantitative formula for solving the knotty problem of how the wishes of the people are to be determined. Moreover, traditions deserve to be re-examined from time to time, particularly when society has changed since they came into being.

What might be called *majoritarian democracy* was adopted when America was a small and primarily agrarian nation, with considerable economic and cultural homogeneity, few conflicting interest groups, and a tradition since rejected that the nonpropertied should have fewer rights than the propertied. As a result, there were fewer serious disputes between majorities and minorities, at least until the Civil War, and majoritarian democracy could be said to have worked. Today, however, America is a highly heterogeneous and pluralistic nation—a society of minority groups, so to speak—and every important political decision requires an intense amount of negotiation and compromise so that enough minorities can be found to create a majority coalition. And even then, America is so pluralistic that not all minorities can be accommodated and some must suffer all the consequences of being outvoted.

America has been a pluralistic society for almost a century, but the shortcomings of majority rule have not become problematic before, mainly because previous generations of outvoted groups had other concerns. The outvoted of the past were also concentrated among poor ethnic and racial minorities, but in earlier years, the economy needed their unskilled labor, so that they had less incentive to confront the majority, except to fight for labor unions. Moreover, they had little reason even to think about majority rule, for government played a smaller role in the economy and in their lives.

Now all this has changed. When governmental policies and appropriations very nearly determine the fate of the poor, the black, draft-age college students, disadvantaged high school students, and not-so-affluent blue-collar workers, such groups must deal with government, and more often than not their demands are frustrated by the workings of majority rule.

Thus it becomes quite pertinent to ask whether majoritarian democracy is still viable, and whether the tradition of majority rule should not be re-examined. If three-fourths of the voters or of a legislative body are agreed on a course of action, it is perhaps hard to argue against majority rule, but what if that rule seriously deprives the other fourth and drives it to disruption? And what if the majority is no more than 55 percent, and consists only of an uneasy and temporary coalition of minorities? Or what if the remaining 45 percent are unable to obtain compromises from the slender majority?

I believe that the time has come to modernize American democracy and adapt it to the needs of a pluralistic society; in short, to create a more *egalitarian* democracy. (I hesitate to use the phrase *pluralistic democracy* only because it has fallen into disrepute from misuse, the present form of democracy in which some but by no means all minority interest groups are able to participate in decision-making having been falsely labeled pluralistic.) A more egalitarian democracy would not do away with majority rule but would require systems of proposing and disposing that took the needs of minorities, powerless and powerful, into consideration, so that when majority rule had serious negative consequences, outvoted minorities would be able to achieve their most important demands and would not be forced to accept tokenism or resort to despair or disruption.

Whenever possible, legislation and appropriation would be based on the principle of "live and let live," with different policies for different groups if consensus and a single policy for all were impossible. Groups of minorities could still coalesce into a majority, but other minorities would be able to choose their own ways of using public power and funds without being punished for it by a majority, particularly when enough resources were available for both the majority and the minority. When resources were scarce, however, then such a solution would be impossible, and other ways would have to be found to prevent majority deprivation of the minorities.

Some Egalitarian Proposals

A book of its own would be necessary to describe how the American political system might be restructured to create a more egalitarian democracy, but I can suggest some specific proposals toward this goal. They fall into two categories: those that incorporate outvoted minorities into the political structure by increasing the responsiveness of governments to the diversity of citizen interests—and to all citizens; and those that restrict majority rule so as to prevent the tyrannization of minorities. These two goals are not always consistent; indeed, more responsiveness would increase the power of the majority, since seniority systems and similar traditions give more power to a minority—though rarely to an outvoted one. However, outvoted minorities must first be brought into the political arena before it is fair to suggest ways of increasing their power. Moreover, many of my proposals have drawbacks—for example, by complicating the political process so as to make decision-making more difficult—and some may be downright unworkable, but I suggest them more to illustrate what needs to be done than to provide immediately feasible solutions. A politically more egalitarian system that also works efficiently is hard to design, and I do not claim to have such a design.

INCREASING GOVERNMENTAL RESPONSIVENESS

The responsiveness of governments can be increased in several ways. First, the "one person, one vote" principle needs to be extended to all levels of government and to the political parties. Obstacles to registering and voting must be removed and legislative bodies at all levels reapportioned to eliminate deliberate gerrymandering of the poor, the black, and other minorities; party leaders, high and low, should be elected by party members; and party candidates should be nominated by primaries or democratically chosen conventions.

Second, the seniority system should be abolished in all legislative bodies, for while someone must lead in such bodies, that role should not automatically go to politicians simply because their own districts re-elect them time after time. Similarly, the power of committee chairmen who may represent only a small number of voters to block legislation wanted by a larger number must be eliminated. Third, the administrative agencies and their bureaucracies must become more accountable, perhaps by replacing appointive officers with elective ones, or by requiring such bodies to be run by elected boards of directors.

Fourth, all election campaigns should be funded by

government, to discourage the near-monopoly that wealthy individuals now have in becoming candidates, and to prevent affluent interest groups from making demands on candidates as a price for financing their campaigns. If equal amounts—and plenty of free television time—were given to all candidates, even from third, fourth, and fifth parties, the diversity of the population would be better represented in the electoral process. This might lead to election by plurality rather than majority, although in a highly diverse community or state such an outcome might not be undesirable, and runoffs could always be required to produce a final majority vote.

Fifth, the representativeness of the country's political representatives can stand improvement, for as I noted in Chapter One, today the 12 percent of Americans who are poor have no representatives in Congress. The poor can be represented by politicians who are not poor, of course, but it would help if they had at least a few spokesmen of their own. If the registered poor could be persuaded to vote in larger numbers, this might happen automatically, but they are not going to be persuaded until they see that voting is a meaningful act for them and that political participation will bring them some benefits. Until this happens, it might be worth while to consider copying the European countries that require all their citizens to vote, provided that voters are free to cast a blank ballot in protest.

Sixth, methods by which the citizenry communicates with its elected representatives ought to be improved. Today, legislators tend to hear only from lobbyists, people in their own social circles, and the writers of letters and newspaper editorials—a highly biased sample of their constituencies. Indeed, the only way an ordinary citizen can communicate is by organizing or writing letters. Of course, such methods make sure that a legislator hears only from deeply interested citizens, protecting him or her from being overwhelmed by too much feedback, but they also discriminate against equally interested people who cannot organize or write. One useful solution is for governments to make postage-free forms available for people who want to write letters to their representatives, to be picked up in banks, post offices, stores, and taverns. Another solution is for governments to finance the establishment of regular but independently run public-opinion polls on every major issue, so that government officials can obtain adequate feedback from a random sample of their constituents, and not only on the few national issues a handful of private pollsters today decide are worth polling about. Yet another solution is for governments to encourage people to organize politically, by allowing them to claim as tax deductions their dues and contributions to lobbying organizations other than political parties. (Limits on the size of such deductions would have to be set to prevent affluent minorities from using their funds to gain extra power; and organizations of the poor, whose members cannot afford to pay dues and do not benefit from tax deductions, could be given government grants if they could prove that two-thirds of their members were poor.)

INCREASING MINORITY POWER

Feasible methods for increasing the power of minorities at the expense of majority rule are more difficult to formulate. One approach is to enhance the power of existing institutions that represent minority interests. If constitutional amendments to establish an economic and racial bill of rights could be passed—for instance, a provision giving every American citizen the right to a job or an income above the poverty line—the power of the poor would be increased somewhat.

Cabinet departments also represent minority interests,

particularly at the federal and state levels, although more often than not they speak for affluent minorities. Nevertheless, if the Office of Economic Opportunity were revived and raised to full cabinet status and a Department of Minorities established in Washington, at least some new legislation and higher appropriations for the poor and the black would result. In other cabinet departments, new bureaus should be set up to represent the interests of outvoted minorities: in the Department of Housing and Urban Development (now dominated by builders and mayors), to look after the needs of slum dwellers; in the Health, Education, and Welfare Department, to deal with the concerns of patients, students, and welfare recipients, respectively. Moreover, the policy-making boards that I suggested earlier to oversee cabinet departments and other administrative agencies should include their clients. Thus, all school boards should include some students; welfare departments, some welfare recipients; and housing agencies, some residents of public housing and projects supported by the Federal Housing Administration.

The financial power of poor minorities could be increased by extending the principles of the progressive income tax and of school-equalization payments to all governmental expenditures. Funding of government programs could be based in part on the incomes of their eventual recipients, so that the lower their income, the higher the government grant. Poorer communities would thus obtain more federal money per capita for all public services, and subsidies for mass-transit programs would automatically be higher than for expressways to suburbia.

In addition, changes in the electoral system would be needed. One solution would be election by proportional representation. Proportional representation has not been popular in America, partly because it wreaks havoc upon

the two-party system, but it is not at all certain any more
whether a pluralistic society is best served by a two-party
system to begin with, particularly if the two parties have
congressional, presidential, and other fairly permanent
factions. Proportional representation by race or income
would go against the American grain, but as long as racial
and economic integration seem unachievable in the near
future, this solution might be more desirable than forcing
the poor or the black to resort to disruption. Actually, a
kind of proportional representation is already practiced in-
formally in many places; in New York City, election slates
have always been balanced to include candidates from the
major ethnic and religious groups. Perhaps some form of
representation by occupation, once proposed by Daniel
De Leon and by the guild socialists, ought to be recon-
sidered, for job concerns are often more important than
community ones in the voters' choices, and the many
workers not represented now by unions or professional
associations have virtually no political voice.

Another approach would restrict majority rule directly
by making all elections and voting procedures in legislative
branches of government go through a two-step process,
with majority rule applying only to the final step. This
system, somewhat like the runoff used in some state and
municipal elections, would require that if any legislative
proposal or appropriation obtains at least 25 percent of the
total vote, it must be revised and voted on again until it is
either approved by a majority or rejected by 80 percent
of the voting body. In the meantime, compromises would
have to be made, either watering down the initial proposal
so that a majority could accept it, or satisfying other demands of the minority through the time-honored practice
of logrolling so that they would allow 80 percent of the
voting body to reject the original proposal. For example,

if at least a quarter of a congressional committee supported a minimum-income grant for the poor, perhaps the second vote would produce at least a weaker version of the tax that the majority could live with. Of course, such a system would work only if outvoted minority groups were able to elect representatives in the first place.[1] Also, it is always possible that legislators who favored a highly regressive income tax or segregationist policies would be able to obtain legislation for their minorities, but if an economic and racial bill of rights were added to the Constitution, such legislation would be thrown out by the courts.

Outvoted minorities could also achieve greater political power by the alteration of existing political boundaries and powers so that they could even become majorities in their own bailiwicks. Proposals for decentralization and community control are boundary-altering schemes with just this political consequence, and some of the disadvantages of these schemes today could be alleviated by my previous proposal for progressive methods of government funding to provide money to poorer communities. But the concept of redrawing boundaries ought to be applied more broadly, for many existing political subdivisions are anachronistic. For example, it is difficult to justify the existence of many of the states as political units today, and it might be useful to think about creating smaller and more homogeneous units in highly urbanized parts of the country, perhaps of county size in order to reduce the number of outvoted minorities. This is a form of community control, to be sure, and it has two serious drawbacks: without a progressive federal funding program, it only gives the poor control over their own poverty; and it disperses central power, for example, the city-wide power of the blacks as they become an urban majority. Thus, boundary-redrawing schemes can increase the power of minorities only if some central decision-making—and sources of power—are retained.

Finally, changes in the rules of the political system must be supplemented by changes in the economic system, for *it* is ultimately a major obstacle to improving the lot of many outvoted minorities—and even of the unorganized majority. Some of my earlier proposals are equally relevant here. The "one person, one vote" principle might be extended to stockholders who elect corporate boards of directors; a cabinet department to represent consumers and other corporate customers should be set up; feedback from stockholders and customers to the corporate "legislature" should be improved, and they as well as workers should sit on corporate boards. In an era when many firms are subsidized by government contracts and tax credits, it is certainly possible to argue that at least such firms should become more democratic.

THE NEED FOR MORE POLITICAL EQUALITY

Most of my proposals are purposely intended to enhance the power of poor and black—and of course, other racial— minorities, for as I noted earlier, this seems to me the only way of solving the problems of the cities and the country. But such a democracy is needed by all minorities who stand in danger of being outvoted by a majority, whatever their income or color. As the current demands of more people for greater equality and more control over their lives increase, and the role of government in society continues to mount at the same time, the need for more political equality will become increasingly urgent. What is so inaccurately described as the urban crisis is in reality the beginning of a national political crisis, but it is also an opportunity for America to develop new ways of living together.

NOTE

This essay is a revised version of "We Won't End the Urban Crisis Until We End Majority Rule," *The New York Times Magazine*, August 3, 1969, pp. 10–15, 20, 24–28.

1. After this article originally appeared, a number of colleagues pointed out, some in print, that my proposal was a restatement of John Calhoun's concept of "concurring majorities." In his attempt to defend the South and Southern slavery against being outvoted by a Northern majority, Calhoun distinguished between an absolute majority, in this case of the country as a whole, and another

> in which [the country] is regarded in reference to its different political interests, whether composed of different classes, of different communities formed into one general confederated community, and in which the majority is estimated, not in reference to the whole, but to each class or community of which it is composed—the assent of each taken separately—and the concurrence of all constituting the majority. A majority thus estimated may be called the concurring majority.

> John C. Calhoun, "Letter to General Hamilton on the Subject of State Interposition," *The Works of John Calhoun,* ed. Richard K. Cralle (New York: Russell & Russell, Publishers, 1968), vol. 6, p. 181.

Although I was not familiar with Calhoun's concept when I wrote the original article, it is somewhat similar to my proposal, for it also attempts to prevent majority tyrannization, albeit in an ignoble cause. I see no reason to question my proposal, as some writers have done, on the grounds of its resemblance to Calhoun's, although it may have other drawbacks. Similar political ideas are often used to achieve different goals, and an idea should be judged in terms of whether it achieves the goal—without serious consequences for other goals—and whether the goal being sought is itself desirable, rather than in terms of its origins.

6
The Possibilities of Income Redistribution

When Senator McGovern's ill-fated campaign for the presidency is remembered in years to come, it will probably be only as the first American presidential campaign of modern times to raise the issue of income redistribution. To be sure, the senator borrowed the idea from Fred Harris' own brief presidential stand and gave it little prominence in his campaigning, but he did place it on the country's political agenda. And even though income redistribution was buried along with everything else in the Nixon landslide, I suspect it will reappear in future presidential campaigns and may someday become the law of the land. Some current trends in the American economy and in people's attitudes toward it suggest that income redistribution is an idea whose time has just about arrived.

TRENDS TOWARD INCOME REDISTRIBUTION

These trends, which I described in detail in Chapters One and Two, particularly on pages 19–20, were set in motion by the rising expectations for a higher standard of living that developed among moderate-income Middle Americans as a result of the affluence that followed World War II. Although the expectations have been frustrated by the economic downturn following the escalation of the Indochinese war, they have not been given up; instead, many Americans believe that government should step in to preserve their standard of living and intervene in the economy for this purpose. Moreover, the ever-heightening fear that automation and other technological changes are reducing the supply of jobs encourages the belief that government must ensure the existence of jobs, particularly in an era when the opportunity to go into business for oneself is also declining for the average American.

In addition, people who once believed that as long as the economy continued to grow, their own incomes would rise accordingly, are now having some doubts, because of the absorption of much of that growth by the large corporations, including multinational ones, the recent decline of growth and the increase in foreign competition, and the ecological arguments for restricting growth.

All these doubts about the ability of the economy—and particularly of private enterprise—to guarantee the achievement of economic expectations are beginning to make people aware of the unequal distribution of wealth and income in America, which in turn made it possible for Senators Harris and McGovern to include redistributional proposals in their 1972 campaigns. At present, this awareness is limited to the fact that many rich individuals and corporations escape the payment of taxes through tax preferences and loopholes; but if current economic trends continue, more people will become aware of other economic inequalities, and eventually some will begin to realize that they can best achieve their own expectations if income and wealth are shared more equally. And when a politically significant number of Americans come to this realization, serious political pressure for income redistribution will begin to develop.

THE POSSIBILITIES OF TAX REFORM

Income can be redistributed from the rich to the rest of the population in several ways: (1) through tax reform; (2) by government programs and subsidies that go to the less affluent but are paid for by the more affluent, such as welfare benefits; (3) by tax-funded government programs such as national health insurance, which replace expensive commercial ones; (4) through educational programs that enable people to obtain better jobs; and (5) through the creation of new jobs, which is especially effective in redistributing income to the unemployed and underpaid. Although the federal income tax has long been viewed as a logical device for redistributing income, it has not functioned that way, for as I indicated in Chapter One, there is virtually no difference between before-tax and after-tax income distributions. Over the years, several attempts at progressive tax reform have all come to nought, partly because of political opposition by affluent individual and corporate taxpayers, and Presidents Kennedy and Nixon contributed further to inequality by corporate tax reductions and new depreciation allowances.

Nevertheless, tax reform has remained the kingpin of

most recent redistributive schemes, and closing the tax loopholes of the rich has been on the agenda of liberals for
many years. Even so, the first fledgling moves toward income redistribution were made to help the poor without
taking from the rich. Antipoverty warriors looking for a
substitute for the welfare system took up Milton Friedman's idea of the Negative Income Tax (NIT) to be paid
out as a cash grant to the nontaxpaying poor, which eventually became part of President Nixon's ill-fated Family
Assistance Plan (FAP). Despite Daniel Patrick Moynihan's
claim that FAP was a radical redistributive scheme, it did
not call for higher taxes on the rich and it proposed a
mere $2,400 minimum grant for a family of four without
other income—so that it would have raised the income of
welfare recipients in only about eight states.[1] Although
FAP also provided a grant to the many working poor who
labor full-time at jobs without earning enough, that grant
would have ended at $3,940 for a four-person family, an
income still below the 1972 federal poverty line of $4,140.

Senator McGovern came up with two redistributive
ideas during his campaign. One was his proposal for taxing
"unearned" income in the same way as "earned," thus
eliminating the tax preferences that come with capital
gains, tax-exempt municipal bonds, and tax shelters for
real estate, among others, all of which benefit mainly the
rich. His second proposal was to give every American a
tax credit of $1,000 a year, but he stated it so badly that
the resulting political protest forced him to withdraw it
shortly afterwards. Actually, that proposal was for a whole
new system of collecting taxes, the Credit Income Tax
(CIT), first invented in England during World War II by
Lady Rhys Williams, then reinvented here by Berkeley
economist Earl Rolph, and further developed by James
Tobin, who later became a McGovern adviser.[2]

The basic idea behind the CIT is simple: it proposes

to tax all income, whether from salaries, capital gains, or any other source, at the same flat rate, thus eliminating both the tax loopholes for the wealthy and the personal exemption now claimed by every taxpayer. Instead the CIT would provide everyone with a tax credit, such as the $1,000 per person Senator McGovern suggested, which would be paid in cash to those persons whose credit exceeded their tax bills, and which would provide a guaranteed minimum-income grant to people without other income. The CIT differs from the NIT in that it applies to everyone, not just the poor and working poor, and it is also more progressive, for the combination of a universal credit and a flat tax rate exempts many moderate-income people from the payment of income taxes and even reduces the tax burden of the slightly more affluent.

For example, a CIT plan grounded on the original McGovern proposal, which Harold Watts, the University of Wisconsin economist, presented to the 1972 Democratic Party Platform Hearings, called for a tax credit of $3,720 for the prototypical family of four and a basic tax rate of 33⅓ percent on all income.[3] Under the Watts plan, the minimal grant in lieu of welfare would have come to $3,720, and the wage earner with $3,940 who would have received nothing further from FAP would have received another $2,407 from CIT, for a total income of $6,347, or 56 percent more than his income from wages. (His tax credit would have been $3,720 minus $1,313, the 33⅓ percent tax on his $3,940 income, which would have been added to his income from wages.) A $6,000 earner would have been eligible for an additional $1,720, which, with the elimination of the $300 income tax he now pays, would have given him a 33⅓ percent increase in income; a $8,000 earner would have received $1,054 and a 22 percent increase in income.[4]

The median-income earner, who now gets just above

$10,000 and pays about $1,000 in federal taxes, would have been eligible for $420 in tax credits, producing a 14 percent increase in total income; and all families earning up to $11,160, at which point the $3,720 is exactly equal to the 33⅓ percent tax on their earnings, would have received some cash payments, as well as relief from present taxes. Since the Watts plan was designed for implementation in 1975 and the median family income is expected to reach $11,000 at that time, roughly half of all Americans would have been freed from paying income taxes and eligible for some tax credit in cash.

The resulting losses in tax receipts would have been made up by more affluent people, particularly those who earned money from capital gains and other tax-preferred sources. For example, a family of four with a $27,500 income, half of which was derived from capital gains, would have been paying almost $5,500 in taxes as compared with $3,150 now; a similar family with a $100,000 income from the same sources, $33,000 instead of $24,300. Families with incomes entirely from salaries or wages would also have paid higher taxes once their incomes reached about $25,000.

The CIT has a number of important virtues in addition to its redistributive potential. First, it would considerably simplify taxpaying and tax collection, since taxpayers would list all their income and then pay the flat rate amount minus the credit. Second, it is flexible, for not only can the flat rate be adjusted to meet national needs, but it can be raised at higher incomes. (Watts, for example, proposed a 40 percent rate for income over $50,000 and a 50 percent rate for income over $100,000.) Also, socially desirable deductions can be retained, such as those for medical and charitable contributions, which Watts kept in his plan. Third, it avoids a major drawback of the NIT, which economists call the "notch problem." Since NIT is tied to the existing tax structure, a tax inequity arises at the income point where NIT stops, for the family with that income pays no tax; but the family with just one dollar more in income pays the regular income tax, thus making its after-tax income somewhat less. Although this problem would not have arisen with FAP because, like the $3,940 earner, the $3,941 earner is exempt from the income tax as a result of tax reforms passed in 1969, it would arise with a NIT which ends at $4,500 or $5,000, and requires setting up a "tax break-even line" with a reduced tax rate to iron out the inequity. Under the CIT, such inequities do not exist, since everyone is taxed at the same rate.

Like all good ideas, the CIT also has some disadvantages. For one thing, it relies on an absolute figure for the minimal grant, which remains static as other people's incomes rise, and would thus further increase the inequality gap between the poor and other Americans that I described in Chapter One. To prevent this, some poverty researchers have advocated that both the poverty line and minimum grants be set at a percentage of median income so that they would rise with increases in median income. Adapting this notion to the Watts plan, the universal tax credit would be set at 37 percent of median income, but this is about $400 below even the current poverty line. Victor Fuchs has argued that the poverty line should be set at 50 percent of median income, and on the basis of Rainwater's analysis of Gallup poll data which I described in Chapter Three, page 67, I believe that it and the tax credit should be set at 60 percent.[5] Consequently, a more redistributive CIT plan designed to reduce the inequality of the poor would begin with a tax credit equal to 60 percent of median income, or about $6,000 in today's income figures as determined by the census—and more if other definitions of income and other data-gathering methods are used. Such a plan would also redistribute more money to moderate-income people, for with a flat tax rate of 33⅓ percent, the $6,000 earner would receive $10,000; the $8,000 earner, $11,334; and the $10,000 earner, $12,667.

Even a high minimal-income grant is still a substitute for welfare, and while it would eliminate poverty and reduce inequality, people who are unable to work would continue to be dependent on government for their income. This dependency is unpopular not only with taxpayers but with most welfare recipients as well; in America, almost everyone believes that income ought to be derived from work. Consequently, the minimum-income grant built into the CIT should be paid only to people clearly unable to work for reasons of ill-health, old age, or familial responsibilities; for the rest of the population, the minimum income, whether set at $3,720 or at 60 percent of median income, should come from a job. The best income-redistribution scheme, particularly for the poor, is therefore a full-employment program, which provides funds to private enterprise to create new and well-paying jobs, and uses the government as an employer of "later resort" until the unemployment rate is down to 2 percent, the standard in most European countries.

A job-based income-redistribution scheme would in effect mean an end not only to unemployment but also to underemployment and low-wage labor in general. It would require a shift from the present capital-intensive trend in industry to a labor-intensive one, but since the job-creating potential of industry has been poor in recent years, most of the new jobs would have to be in the public services, whether privately or publicly administered. It would be possible to create such jobs in many services—education, health, mental health, and recreation—as well as to raise the quality of other public services, from garbage pickup to cleaning up America's polluted rivers.

At the same time, however, wages would have to be increased in many existing private firms and public agencies, and those among the former which can only survive with low-wage labor would either have to raise their prices to the consumer or go out of business. Consequently, it may be impossible to redistribute income solely through the creation of better jobs and what is in effect a much higher minimal wage; most likely, some combination of job-creation and tax-credit schemes would be necessary, the latter then functioning as a kind of wage supplement. And if not all able-bodied people who wanted to work could find jobs, they would have to receive a minimal-income grant instead.

THE ECONOMIC EFFECTS OF INCOME REDISTRIBUTION

Income redistribution cannot be treated as an end in itself; it is only a means to the improvement of society and the general welfare, and one must therefore consider whether it would lead to the needed improvement, and whether it would have other effects that would only make things worse. The first question is obviously about its economic effects: Could the economy afford either the Watts plan or the more redistributive proposal that combines jobs with a minimal grant set at 60 percent of median income (hereafter to be called the 60 percent plan); and if so, who would be benefitted and who would be hurt, and most important, what would happen to incentives to work and to invest?

That the economy can afford income redistribution in the abstract is not difficult to document, for as I noted in Chapter One, if national Total Personal Income were divided equally, the prototypical family of four would receive close to $17,000, more than half again the current median income. More concretely, Watts has shown that his plan would be entirely feasible: after tax credits had been paid, it would raise $129 billion in taxes, which, together with the savings of $18 billion from the elimination of public assistance and other transfer payments, would yield $147 billion dollars, enough to meet the Brookings Institution estimate of $144 billion dollars to be raised from personal income taxes in 1975. The 60 percent plan is another matter; it would cost about $100 billion more in additional taxes, and while some funds could be raised by increasing the flat tax rate on high incomes, the rest would have to come from a redistribution of wealth, and not just annual income.

In reality, of course, tax reform does not "cost" anything extra; it only redistributes existing tax bills, and while the new tax bills would be considered costs by the affluent, they would be benefits for the rest of the population. Job-creation programs however, would, require higher governmental expenditures, and these would have to come out of somebody's taxes, but some of the initial expenditures would come back to the government as the taxes resulting from the higher productivity generated by full employment. Even service jobs would have such an effect; for example, a higher level of health services would alleviate one cause of industry absenteeism and thus increase productivity in manufacturing.

The principal beneficiaries of CIT would be poor and moderate-income Americans; as already indicated, the Watts plan would relieve almost half the population of federal income taxes and provide it with some cash benefits from the tax credit. The principal losers would be people who derived most of their income from capital gains and other tax-preferred sources, for example, those making their living playing the stock market. The very rich among them would pay the highest tax increase, but it would constitute only a small proportion of their income. Conversely, such people in the $25,000 to $50,000 income bracket might lose a more sizable proportion of their income to the tax collector. Their number is small, however; projecting from a 1962 study, families in that income bracket receive only about 12 percent of their total income from property ownership and not all of it would be affected by the Watts plan.[6] Census data for 1970 showed that only 0.8 percent of families then in that income bracket— 17,000 families in the entire country—reported obtaining their income entirely from sources other than salaries, and again, many of these sources would not be affected by the CIT reform.[7]

The prime question about income redistribution has to do with its impact on the economy, and particularly on incentives of the poor to work if they could make a living from a $3,720 or $6,000 tax credit, and on the incentives of the rich to work and invest if taxes ate up more of their incomes. McGovern's tax-reform proposals predictably set off a series of gloomy predictions on all these questions from Wall Street, rich campaign contributors, and conservative journalists and intellectuals. Their main worry was that incentives would be so seriously damaged that the economy would be plunged into a major depression; in fact, Pierre Renfret, an economic pollster who sometimes advises President Nixon, quickly reported that 43 percent of the businessmen he sampled said that they would reduce their capital-investment plans after hearing the McGovern proposals.

These reactions should not be surprising, for the beneficiaries of the current tax system would sustain some losses, and their understandable opposition is easily translated into dire predictions. They might even be right in the short run, insofar as tax reform would set off a panic on their part, creating fears about the future that would become a self-fulfilling prophecy by affecting their actions in the present. But since no tax reform scheme with income-redistribution potential could be implemented without a long political struggle, its opponents could, if they were not able to prevent it, make preparations for living with it, and learn that in the long run, at least, their fears were not justified.

Conventional economic thinking would of course argue that these fears are justified even for the long run, for as I indicated in Chapter Three, pages 84–89, the economic rationality that underlies such thinking assumes that people do not like to work, would not work if they could obtain a CIT income grant instead, and would not work as hard if their after-tax incomes went down or invest if their after-tax profits were cut. Conversely, common sense and a good deal of sociological research have suggested that people work also to feel socially useful and to obtain self-respect, that the poor share these feelings, that even welfare recipients want to work, and that their work incentive is increased when they are given economic aid.

Their incentive to take underpaid, insecure, and dirty jobs would, however, be considerably reduced if they could obtain an equivalent and more secure income from a tax-credit grant. Indeed, during the congressional debate on FAP, Senator Russell Long was quoted in the press as asking who would launder his shirts if his laundress could get a $2,400 FAP grant instead, and the Nixon administration included a workfare provision in FAP in order to force poor people to take such jobs.

As for the affluent, studies indicate that tax increases make people work harder and longer to bring their take-home pay back up to the previous level. Older people might not work so hard if they could not pass as much of their fortune on to their children, but this should not affect productivity, for owners of family firms would just pass the reins on to their children at a younger age and corporation presidents would retire a little earlier.

Occupations that cater largely to the rich might suffer from tax reform, not in the loss of incentive, but in the loss of reward; painters and sculptors, for example, would lose some sales if the rich had to pay higher taxes. While this would not discourage people from entering the arts, since their motivation for doing so is not primarily economic, it would force the few who can now make a living from their work to take other jobs, as most artists do even today, although a wise society would increase public subsidies to museums so as to compensate artists for the loss of private customers.

As I suggested on pages 89–90, the incentive to take risks with one's money is more affected by rational economic motives than work, but even investment is a social process. Private investors invest not only to make a profit but to make more profit than other private investors, and as long as the opportunity to make more profit than anyone else is available, investors will continue to invest, even if the over-all level of profit is reduced by tax reform. In addition, being an investor is an occupation in itself and is thus governed by some of the social and emotional motives that go with work.

Nevertheless, if a CIT plan were adopted and tax preferences for capital gains were eliminated, people earning less than $50,000 a year would have less incentive—and less money—to invest; their now-reduced income would go into consumption. The very rich, who are the most important private investors, cannot consume much more than they already do, and they would have to continue to be investors, even if they were unhappy about a lower after-tax profit. They might look instead for new sources of high-profit investment, including foreign and illegitimate ones, and the government would have to make sure that such sources were either taxed more heavily or otherwise restricted.

The stock market would undoubtedly decline with the onset of the CIT and the fear that the rich would stop investing, but stock prices would rise again, if not to their present levels, once this fear was shown to be groundless. Moreover, with only 5 percent of corporate capital requirements now coming from the stock market, even a temporary panic in the stock market would not endanger the economy as a whole. Still, that market plays an important symbolic role in the economy, providing a simple if not exactly reliable indicator of economic health, and before tax reform could be instituted, private enterprise and government would have to develop a new index to replace the Dow-Jones and other stock-market indicators by which investors could gauge the national economic health and the profit potential of their investment alternatives.

Corporate incentives to invest would not be significantly reduced by the CIT because corporations need to continue to grow and to prevent their competitors from obtaining a larger share of the market. Among small and family-owned firms, the CIT might depress investment incentives, but among large oligopolistic corporations, the major effect would be some reluctance to make extremely risky investments. This can be counteracted by appropriate increases in selected depreciation allowances, by additional government investment subsidies, and even by over-all reductions in the corporate tax rate, as long as such reductions were made only to ensure against a loss of productivity and employment.

Tax reform might, however, discourage some non-profit investment, that is, donations to nonprofit institutions such as museums and universities, particularly on the part of people earning less than $50,000, who would presumably offset their higher taxes by cutting down on charitable contributions rather than by giving up luxuries to which they have become accustomed. Nonprofit and charitable institutions that depend heavily on the largesse of such people might be hurt, but since the CIT does not require the repeal of the tax deduction for charitable contributions, it seems unlikely that the very rich would forgo the prestige —and also the immortality—that accompanies large donations to cultural institutions. In fact, they might be encouraged to give more if the CIT were complemented by a more stringent inheritance tax.

Yet even if such donations should decrease, one can argue that privately owned nonprofit institutions are in reality public, and should be financed by the public through the federal government rather than be dependent on the whims of rich philanthropists. Admittedly, the federal government will not be eager to fund private universities or museums while public agencies are demanding more money; also, in a society with as high an infant mortality rate as ours, one can argue that government funds for further museum acquisitions are less urgent than better health care. Besides, inheritance and other tax laws could be rewritten so that monies from the very rich and from old fortunes would flow into foundations like those established by the Fords, Rockefellers, Carnegies, and others, particularly to finance cultural and other activities that are too controversial or politically unprofitable for government financing.

Finally, the deflationary effects of higher taxes on the

rich would be offset by the additional economic activity generated by the beneficiaries of the CIT and of job-creation programs. Not only is full employment a better stimulus to investment than income inequality, but both poor and moderate-income consumers will generate additional economic activity by buying more goods and services, and the latter will put some money into savings which can be invested in place of the reluctant capital of the rich. No one can estimate now the additional GNP, tax receipts, and new jobs which would be created as multiplier effects from the CIT alone, but while Seventh Avenue might sell fewer $500 dresses, it would sell many more at $25.

THE SOCIAL EFFECTS OF INCOME REDISTRIBUTION

The effects of income redistribution on American society would probably be more dramatic than those on the economy, for even the Watts plan would free the approximately 7 million families now earning less than $3,720, and the 2 million individuals earning less than the $1,320 tax credit Watts has proposed for individuals, from much of the constant worry, stress, and depression that go with being poor, enabling them to live with somewhat more joy, dignity, and self-respect. This in turn would reduce some of the current tension and conflict between the haves and the have-nots. At first, these effects might be less visible than complaints about higher taxes by rich speechmakers and columnists, but as the morale of the poor began to rise, so would that of the rest of the population, particularly in communities with sizable poor populations. The Watts plan would also make possible the elimination of public welfare, and thus liberate its recipients from the harsh regulations and the stigma under which they now live, and it might even reunite some broken families now separated by AFDC regulations. Even so, the total number of female-headed families, black and white, would probably not change, since the $3,720 minimum income would give other mothers enough economic independence not to marry, especially if job opportunities for poor males were not improved at the same time.

The most startling impact of the Watts plan would be felt in the nonurban sections of America, the South and other poor regions, for there the economic gap between the poor and their neighbors would be narrowed. In the South, for example, where the median income is $1,500 less than that of the nation—and of its other regions—a poor person receiving $3,720 would now obtain over 40 percent of the median income, as compared with about one-tenth to one-fourth the median obtained by welfare recipients at present. Consequently, many of the poor would be able to improve their standard of living and spruce up their homes, or to move out of the slums, particularly in areas where rents are still low. In addition, the recipients of CIT grants would funnel additional monies into the economies of nonurban and poor regions, and thus contribute to their general economic improvement.

These improvements should in turn stem the migration of the poor to the cities, lessening some of the city's financial problems and social tensions. (The Puerto Rican migration to the United States would, however, rise to fantastic heights, unless the Watts plan were also implemented there.) Some urban welfare recipients might even return "home," where their $3,720 would provide a higher standard of living. Narrowing the inequality gap between the poor and the more affluent residents of these areas could create new social conflict, however, for the latter might feel that as the poor improved their living conditions they would also become "uppity" and no longer pay them the deference they now receive. For example, since added income usually results in more political influence, the beneficiaries of the CIT might seek to participate in community activities from which they are now excluded and demand a greater say in community politics. The resulting tensions would be particularly strong in the South, where many of the beneficiaries would be blacks, and it is possible that more affluent white Southerners would make life so unpleasant for them that they would move North, even at some economic disadvantage.

In the large cities that now pay liberal welfare benefits, the Watts plan would not significantly increase the incomes of welfare recipients; in New York, for example, some recipients already get over $4,000 a year—although most cities are not that generous. The CIT would, however, increase the incomes of those poor people who are not eligible for welfare or who, despite their eligibility, are not receiving it because of the cutback on welfare expenditures. Consequently, CIT should contribute to rising standards of living among the urban poor as well. This should be accompanied by some improvements in their health, though only if current health programs for the poor are maintained or if national health insurance replaces them; $3,720 is not enough of an income to buy decent medical care in the private market. Similarly, some people would be able to leave the slums, though fewer than in small cities, but again, only if subsidized housing programs were continued and enlarged, for in the big cities $3,720 is not enough income to pay the rent outside (or inside) the slums.

Both in and out of the cities, reductions in some of the

pathologies associated with poverty—alcoholism, drug addiction, and mental illness—could be expected, and crime motivated by economic need alone should drop. Higher incomes, combined with recent improvements in drug treatment, might make it possible to reduce the number of drug addicts and alcoholics, although many of the addicted—as of the mentally ill—are probably beyond help. The major effect of the Watts proposal would be to lessen the despair that recruits people into escape-seeking addictions and illnesses, and the number of new addicts should decline. Fewer addicts would also result in a little less crime, both in the slums and in more affluent neighborhoods, and it is even possible that the streets and parks of the city would be somewhat safer than they have been for a long time.

Nevertheless, the redistribution called for by the Watts plan would not be enough to bring about a significant decline in these pathologies. A $3,720 income would enable mothers to buy their children the kind of clothing they need to go to school without feeling inferior, but it would not be enough to reduce other, more serious inequalities or the feelings about them. Pathology and crime would probably decline significantly only with full employment and the more drastic redistributive scheme I described as the 60 percent plan, and even then progress would be slow, for not only would it take some time to heal the emotional ravages of a heritage of inequality, but more equality would generate higher expectations and demands for the removal of other sources of inequality.

Moderate-income families would, as already indicated, benefit from the Watts plan both through the tax credit and through relief from present taxes, ranging from a net increase in income of 33⅓ percent among $6,000 earners to 8 percent among $12,000 earners. The Watts plan would thus enable them to raise their standard of living by the same proportion, although it would not be enough for a major change in life-style, except among the $6,000 to $8,000 earners. Besides, more money alone will not lead working-class families to stop entertaining the relatives around the kitchen table or in the family room and hold formal cocktail parties instead. Ambitious families might be able to send one of their children to a better college than originally planned, thus enabling some of them to move into the professional middle class, but many more would put the extra money into various consumer goods and better housing. Many of the remaining city dwellers would try to join the suburban trek, although a greater degree of income redistribution would be necessary before most were able to afford suburbia's ever more costly housing.

Black moderate-income families would perhaps benefit from the same tax credit more than whites, for many would use it to escape the slums, and those who could head for the suburbs would have easier access to the better jobs located there. Although most would undoubtedly wind up in suburban ghettos, their higher incomes would also increase the size of the black middle class, and this, together with the benefits going to the poor, might begin to lessen the racial discrimination among whites which is based on fears of lower-class pathology and rests on the now accurate generalization that many blacks are lower class. Nevertheless, a black middle class of sufficient size to make real inroads into discrimination could come only with a higher degree of redistribution.

Among the affluent, the effects of the Watts plan would be felt only by people who can now buy extra luxuries with the profits from capital gains and other tax-preferred sources. Some would have to give up some of these luxuries, particularly people in the $25,000 to $50,000 bracket who depend on tax-preferred income for the luxuries they can afford, and they might have to forgo an extra European trip or a more expensive summer home. The tax increases they would experience under the CIT would not be high enough to affect their over-all style of life, however; they would not have to take their children out of private schools or give up the second or third car. The very rich would pay much higher taxes, of course, but since they can afford them, their style of life would not be touched at all. Perhaps high and café society would become a little more austere, additional large mansions might be sold to suburban developers, and some gentlemen farmers might have to give up their rural holdings if these no longer served as tax shelters.

Still, these changes would be noticed mainly on the society pages and among some of the fanciest stores. Indeed, the principal impact of the Watts CIT scheme on the rich would most likely be psychological; some might panic that they were henceforth condemned to relative poverty, even if their panic was groundless. They might also feel that their social and political influence on American society would decline sharply, although that feeling would be groundless as well. Only a much higher degree of income redistribution could have such an effect.

THE POLITICAL PROSPECTS OF REDISTRIBUTION

Neither the economic nor the social effects of income redistribution, particularly that called for by the Watts plan, are likely to result in serious or long-term problems, but the fears of economic decline which income redistribution is already evoking suggest that even as moderate a scheme as Watts's would arouse considerable political opposition.

The rich will argue strenuously that they should not be required to share their hard-earned wealth, and that income redistribution poses a threat to everyone, rich or poor, who still has hopes of becoming rich. They may even suggest that government has no right to interfere with anyone's pursuit of wealth, even though government already interferes, by tax preferences and by subsidizing college educations, housing mortgages, and other goods and services which add to people's income, especially that of the rich.

Consequently, when income redistribution returns to the political agenda, it is doubtful that the poor, who would be its major beneficiaries, will be able to put enough pressure on Congress to overcome the objections of the rich or to quiet the fears about the economy. Most labor unions, in the past the most stalwart lobbyists for progressive domestic legislation, would probably support a scheme like the Watts plan, and so would many liberals, but they are not politically strong enough to exert the needed pressure, either alone or in coalition with organizations of the poor.

As a result, the fate of income redistribution lies in the hands of the people who constitute the moderate-income majority. When they are actively interested in a piece of legislation, they can pass or defeat almost anything, but at present, income redistribution is so new an idea in America that most of them are completely unfamiliar with it. When Senator McGovern first issued his tax-credit proposal, their unfamiliarity quickly turned to hostility; Senator McGovern's failure to explain the proposal and Senator Humphrey's misrepresentation of it were persuasive enough that even potential beneficiaries perceived it only as a new and higher dole to welfare recipients for which they would bear the costs. Their reaction was not entirely irrational; many moderate-income people are opposed to higher benefits for the nonworking poor, and they are even opposed to tax reform per se, for they fear that they will have to pay the largest share of the new taxes, as they often have in the past.

Consequently, it is impossible to predict how the majority of Americans will react to income redistribution until it again becomes a political issue and they have become familiar with it. At this point, its fate will depend also on how the news media deal with it, for not only will most Americans get their knowledge of income redistribution from these media, but politicians often measure the public reaction to an idea by how they report it and editorialize about it. Owners of newspapers and television stations, most of whom are rich or Republican or both, are unlikely to favor income redistribution, and even many journalists, most of whom have only recently become affluent enough to play the stock market, are not likely to be enthusiastic. Despite their unquestioned allegiance to objectivity and fairness in reporting the news, they could unconsciously insert their own misgivings into the questions they ask of their sources, or find the opponents of redistribution more dramatic and newsworthy than its advocates.

Nevertheless, uncomplimentary news stories and hostile editorials will not prevent moderate-income people from supporting income redistribution once they realize that it will mean additional money in their pockets. At the same time, it is perfectly possible that they will not support a plan that increases the income of the poor or ameliorates the harsh conditions under which welfare is given out. This is suggested by the defeat of FAP and the continuing indication in opinion polls that many people still feel the poor are to blame for their own poverty and that too much is already being done for blacks. On the other hand, a recent study by Lee Rainwater of popular reactions to FAP among Bostonians found that many members of his sample not only favored it but came out for a higher minimal grant than anyone has yet proposed, and were even willing to pay higher taxes for it. Their generosity was based on the notion "that FAP would provide higher benefits for families than is now the case and therefore truly assist them to have a decent life, provide strong incentives to work and therefore discourage welfare chiseling and laziness, and do so in a straightforward and non-stigmatizing manner."[8] Of course, answers to a sociologist's interview questions do not always predict how people will feel when an idea is actually up before Congress, and besides, those who support it may not exert as much political pressure as its opponents. Consequently, a politically feasible income-redistribution scheme is likely to favor moderate-income Americans and the working poor, providing the unemployed and unemployable poor a modest guaranteed income at best, and a continuation of welfare and workfare at worst.

Even the prospects of that kind of redistribution scheme depend on the economic and political conditions prevailing when the idea resurfaces as an issue, and on the leadership provided by its advocates. If President Nixon follows the normal Republican *modus operandi* during the rest of his second term and opts for a deflationary economic policy that will increase unemployment, particularly among Middle Americans, and if he cannot stop the continuing increases in the cost of living, political pressure for income redistribution is likely to develop faster than it would in prosperous times. In fact, the next Democratic presidential candidate might then give redistribution a central place in his campaign.

Nevertheless, the urgent needs of the poor will have to be met in other ways. As long as most Americans believe that income should be derived from work and as long as they favor policies which put people to work rather than on the dole, the poor are most likely to obtain higher incomes through programs for full employment and deliberate job creation. Such programs must therefore be part of the legislative package when the time comes for America to adopt income redistribution.

From a longer perspective, that legislative package is still only a first step, for eventually America must also consider the redistribution of wealth.[9] Unequal income rests on a foundation of unequal wealth, and some day that foundation must be dismantled by such policies as the breakup of old fortunes, the levying of stricter inheritance taxes, the sharing of unredistributed corporate wealth, and the dispersion of stock ownership. If income redistribution ever becomes politically feasible, the need for greater sharing of the wealth will soon be apparent, and if Americans feel that wealth which is not derived from work does not deserve the same protection as income which *is* derived from work, policies for redistributing wealth may gain a more widespread political acceptance than policies for redistributing income.

NOTES

This essay was written especially for this volume.

1. Daniel P. Moynihan, *The Politics of A Guaranteed Income* (New York: Random House, 1973).
2. Earl Rolph, "A Credit Income Tax," in Theodore Marmor, ed., *Poverty Policy* (Chicago: Aldine Publishing Co., 1972), pp. 207–18;

and James Tobin, "Raising the Incomes of the Poor," in Kermit Gordon, ed., *Agenda for the Nation* (Washington: Brookings Institution, 1968), pp. 77–116.

3. Harold Watts, "Income Redistribution: How It Is and How It Can Be," unpublished paper for the Democratic Platform Hearings, St. Louis, June 17, 1972.

4. Among homeowners, however, all net increases in income computed here would be reduced somewhat by the elimination of homeowners' deductions for taxes and interest payments. Estimates of current tax payments are taken from Russell Lidman, "Cost and Distributional Implications of McGovern's Minimal Income Grant Proposal" (Madison: University of Wisconsin Institute for Research on Poverty, June 1972), tables 10 and 12.

5. Victor Fuchs, "Redefining Poverty and Redistributing Income," *The Public Interest,* no. 8 (Summer 1967), pp. 88–95.

6. In 1962, all families then in the $25,000 to $50,000 bracket received 17 percent of their income from property ownership; families then in the $15,000 to $25,000 bracket, 7 percent. My estimate is based on an average of these two figures. The study is reported in D. Projector, G. Weiss, and E. Thoreson, "Composition of Income as Shown by the Survey of Financial Characteristics of Consumers," in Lee Soltow, ed., *Six Papers on the Size Distribution of Wealth and Income* (New York: National Bureau of Economic Research and Columbia University Press, 1969), p. 122.

7. Computed from Bureau of the Census, *Income in 1970 of Families and Persons in the United States,* Current Population Reports, series P 60, no. 80, tables 16 and 41.

8. Lee Rainwater, "Public Responses to Low Income Policies: FAP and Welfare," unpublished manuscript, February 1972, p. 12; and *What Money Buys* (New York: Basic Books, forthcoming).

9. Alan Steinberg, "The Case for a Wealth Tax," *Social Policy,* vol. 3 (March–April 1973), pp. 51–4.

III
EQUALITY RESEARCH
AND
UTOPIAN SCENARIOS

INTRODUCTION

The final part of the book is written for researchers and utopians, respectively. Chapter Seven lists and discusses some of the social science research necessary for the achievement of more equality, including studies to identify and analyze egalitarian relationships and groups already existing in America, such as friendship. Chapter Eight proposes and illustrates a very different kind of research: the construction of utopian scenarios that describe the outcomes of different kinds of complete equality. These scenarios attempt, very primitively, to outline what societies with complete equality would look like and what problems they would face.

The societies that emerge from these scenarios are not always completely egalitarian and are by no means perfect in other respects, but they are preferable to existing societies. It is, of course, possible to design completely egalitarian utopias, but they come out as small, homogeneous, self-sufficient, and static communities without much division of labor and thus with a fairly low standard of living—and I do not believe anyone in today's America really wants to live in pastoral or primitive stasis. My favorite utopia among those few that are egalitarian as well as modern is that described in Edward Bellamy's brilliant novel, *Looking Backward,* but it has three drawbacks. It calls for more regimentation that modern Americans would stand for; its political system is dominated by a meritocratic though altruistic elite; and above all, it assumes an infinity of resources. Bellamy was writing in the 1880s and was absolutely convinced that his brand of socialism would be not only more humane but also more efficient than the robber-baron capitalism under which he was living. As a result, he took it on faith that no resource would ever be scarce again, hardly a viable assumption even in utopia.

Utopian speculation is as useful as it is enjoyable, and I think it ought to be done much more often, even by social scientists. I also view these scenarios as heuristic models, for a description of the consequences of complete equality offers at least some leads to the possible consequences of more equality and thus puts into sharper perspective some of the policy problems and issues that will come up in planning for egalitarian change in a real society.

7
Some Proposals for Research on Equality

American sociologists have always devoted a great deal of attention to inequality, although by and large they have studied it under another label, social stratification. Conversely, they have almost entirely ignored equality, both as a theoretical and as an empirical topic, displaying little curiosity about whether it exists at all and if not, why not. There are some notable exceptions: the classic article by Davis and Moore, which sought functional justification for inequality, evoked some egalitarian responses from a number of sociologists;[1] a lively and still growing empirical literature exists on the *kibbutz* and on egalitarian policies in Communist countries;[2] and a new literature is developing around the rise of the communes.[3]

This chapter explores the possibilities for further research on equality, and along two lines. It suggests studies that would identify and analyze egalitarian relationships and groups that already exist in American society, and then goes on to propose studies exploring some of the observations presented in earlier chapters. Research to clarify and help solve the problems of equality described in Chapter Three is especially necessary, both for current advocates of more equality and for future policy-makers.

Existing Egalitarian Relationships and Groups

Although most relationships, groups, and institutions in modern society are to some degree unequal, there are also some that are egalitarian, or at least relatively so, and research could be undertaken by identifying these, describing how they work, and explaining why they are egalitarian. Probably the first step in such a research program would be to review all of the major institutions and relationships of society so as to make a list of those which seem to be egalitarian; the second step would be to verify their egalitarian status and analyze the hows and whys of their equality.

I have not made such a list, but egalitarian relationships do exist, although mainly at the micro-level of society. For example, looking back now on my past research in suburbia, I am struck by the fact that neighbor relations among the homeowners of Levittown whom I studied were often quite egalitarian, in the sense that there was little competition for power or status among neighbors—though of course not among all neighbors—and that people exchanged sociability and mutual aid as relative equals. The reasons for this outcropping of equality are not hard to find; for one thing, people tended to establish relationships mainly with neighbors of roughly equal income and age and avoided them with more or less affluent and significantly older or younger ones. As a result, some major impediments to an egalitarian relationship were eliminated almost by definition. Second, the people involved were primarily lower middle class, and status-seeking was not a major item in their culture. Third, the block within which most neighborly relations were pursued was not a social or political unit; it had no incentive to act as a unit and so there was no reason for anyone to be in a position of authority or leadership. In the community I studied, at least, the block acted as a social unit only in order to maintain a respectable front to the outside world, particularly in the care of front lawns. In this area of life, leaders did emerge, particularly those expert enough at lawn care to show new homeowners how to bring their lawns up to the group standard, but their leadership was defined and restricted by this standard. The really expert gardeners who brought their lawns far above the standard were treated as rate-busters. People wanted their lawns to look no better and no worse than anyone else's, partly because they wanted the block to present a common image to outsiders, partly because they had no desire to be scorned either for showing off or for despoiling the block image, and partly because they did not want to do any extra work on the lawn. Their motives may have been impelled by conformity, although that conformity had a purpose and was neither mindless nor sheeplike, but the outcome was egalitarian, even though no one thought of it that way.

Finally, neighbor relations were egalitarian because they were both important and unimportant. They were important because neighbors depended on each other for mutual aid in case of emergencies, minor and major, setting up an exchange system in which neighbors reciprocated in the giving of aid so that, ideally, no one gave more than he or she received. Neighbors, especially women, also exchanged information and particularly therapeutic information about their problems, and since none were or wanted to be experts—for example, on child-rearing or the treatment of husbands—they helped each other as nonexpert equals. In all other respects, however, neighboring was unimportant; it consisted of superficial sociability relationships, which did not become means to important goals, serve crucial needs, or require a large outlay of time or effort. In other words, they were not significant enough to be transformed into unequal relationships.

Another relationship that may often be egalitarian is friendship, particularly close friendship, because it satisfies deep human needs that cannot be satisfied by an unequal exchange. Of course, some people choose friends among people of higher status and are willing to place themselves in an inferior position to derive the status rewards that come with such a relationship, but close friendship depends on the ability to exchange trust, confidences, and socially and otherwise costly kinds of mutual aid; it probably requires self-selection of people who are equal in class, age, and basic values, which in turn makes possible an egalitarian relationship. The equality of friendship is also enhanced by the fact that friendship is not a goal-oriented activity, and that a dyad is not an organized group that must carry out specific tasks. If this hypothesis is correct, then egalitarian relationships should also be found among other groups that operate without specific tasks, such as groups organized around some leisure-time activity, provided it is not a competitive game in which there can be winners and losers or record-makers.

Close friendship satisfies some of the same social and emotional functions as love, and there may be kinds of love relationships in which the partners are equal. Generally speaking, however, lovers are not equals, partly because men and women are more different than friends of the same sex, partly because the sexes are not yet treated equally by the larger society, and partly because family life requires the carrying out of specific tasks which require a division of labor, and which in turn can give rise to inequalities of tasks and of authority.

All of the relationships I have described so far are micro-level and personal; they exist to carry out emotional and expressive functions rather than instrumental, goal- and task-oriented functions, and are probably as egalitarian as they are for these reasons. Undoubtedly other relationships and groups are similar in these respects and might, on further research, turn out to be egalitarian.

At the macro-level, and among impersonal and instrumental relationships, equality is probably much rarer. Nevertheless, it is worthwhile looking here as well. For example, I suspect that relatively egalitarian relationships are established among people of very high status, who therefore have little need for more status-seeking, provided they do not come from the same occupation, particularly if it is competitive at the top. Thus, a gathering of eminent scientists might be egalitarian, as long as they were drawn from different disciplines and sciences that are not competing with each other. Following this line of reasoning, one would expect a good deal of equality among the most upper of upper-class people, since they have achieved all the status that can be achieved, and perhaps also among the most lower of lower-class people, as long as they have all made peace with the fact that they are at the very bottom of society.

The kinds of relationships I have just described suffer from being hypothetical; neither eminent scientists from different disciplines nor the most upper of the upper class often come together. However, there may be impersonal, instrumental relationships that can be found regularly, for example, among occupations involved in a symbiotic exchange with neither having power over the other, such as different medical specialists who refer cases to each other, or a song writer and a lyricist working together on the score and libretto for a musical.

Sociologists of work and the professions can undoubtedly suggest other such occupational relationships, and similar patterns may exist in some nonoccupational relationships. A different and perhaps more fruitful research venture, however, would be to study those groups which are deliberately attempting to reform previously inegalitarian occupational and other groups on an egalitarian basis, such as group medical practices, clinics, community development corporations, law communes, and publications now being set up by young or radical professionals. For example, *Ms.*, the women's magazine, is put together by an editorial collective, without any editorial hierarchy. Research would be useful to determine whether the egalitarian goals of such groups are being realized, and if so, why; and if not, why not. One would also want to know in what respects the groups are egalitarian; whether the division of labor has been abolished, and if so, how; and if not, whether onerous tasks and authority roles are shared or rotated; what temptations toward differentiation of financial and status rewards exist and how they are being combatted; and last but hardly least, whether the success of the egalitarian venture is a result of the recruitment of ideologically committed participants, or whether people without prior egalitarian values can also be incorporated into an egalitarian structure. This kind of research can also be done in the various kinds of residential communes that have been founded in recent years, where it could draw on the previously mentioned *kibbutz* research literature.

Finally, although equality at the macro-level, or societal equality, is hard to find in a modern society, it may be worthwhile studying preindustrial or so-called primitive societies, either through reviewing the existing literature or through new fieldwork, to find out if any are egalitarian, and if so, why. Very simple and small societies without a division of labor can perhaps be egalitarian, particularly if they have no religion or one that does not need priestly authorities; and if they live in an environment where food and shelter are available in unlimited quantity so that the need for private property does not emerge and society does not need to be divided into haves and have-nots. Even some division of labor may not militate against equality; for example, a society in which the men hunt and the women gather fruits or vice versa could be egalitarian as long as both types of food were of equal importance to the society and neither was harder to obtain than the other. Presumably such societies must also be isolated from each other and the outside world; once they establish contact with others, they probably have to generate leaders to negotiate with the outsiders and warriors to defend themselves against hostile ones. I do not know whether studies of such societies would be at all relevant to modern societies, but it seems to me worth some research effort to find out.

RESEARCHING THE POSSIBILITIES AND PROBLEMS OF EQUALITY

The most important research, at least from a policy perspective, would try to estimate from knowledge about existing societies how to deal with the possibilities and problems of equality I discussed earlier in this book. To begin with, a study of the interest groups and movements whose demands require more equality should be undertaken to find out how intense their demands are, and how likely it is that they will be expressed politically in the years to come, and if so, what political consequences are predictable, including the possibility of more equality. This would also require an assessment of the flexibility of the existing polity and economy, to determine whether they can adapt to egalitarian demands or whether more widespread and intense class and other conflicts without significant change are more likely. The same kind of research is necessary on the nature of American expectations I described in Chapter Two.

These studies would really ask whether Americans are ready for equality, even if it comes as an unintended consequence of other demands, but at the same time, research is needed on how different Americans feel about various kinds of equality as a goal of social policy; and whether pro or con, how intense their feelings are and how ready they are to exert political pressure on their behalf. Some studies could be done by interpreting and extrapolating from existing polling research; others would replicate and expand Rainwater's survey in Boston, which I mentioned in Chapter Six. Other studies would need to investigate the extent to which people actually continue to strive for self-improvement or upward mobility, and how and where their striving supports or conflicts with egalitarian tendencies and possibilities. For example, among the now disadvantaged, it is important to know whether they want to reach the income level of the next "highest" socio-economic aggregate, or that of the modal population that practices the standard of living described by Rainwater's idea of the standard package, or that of the most affluent members of society. One would also want to know whether they seek only a particular income level, or whether they also want the life-style and status which go along with that income level—and since different people want different things, one would need to find out who wants each of these alternatives.

One of the problems of equality I discussed in Chapter Three is possible conflict with incentives, and an income-redistribution policy cannot be properly framed until more is known about how people at all levels of the income hierarchy would react to changes in their income, downward as well as upward. More research is also needed on the noneconomic motivations for work, on the willingness of poor people to do "dirty" work if they can obtain incomes in lieu of work, and conversely, on the behavior of more affluent people as workers (and investors) when their rewards are reduced. Since taxes are going up all the time, especially at local and state levels, opportunities for empirical fieldwork are nearly infinite, and other studies could be made of the impact of indirect taxation, such as inflation. Economists need to mount theoretical and empirical studies of the macro-effects on productivity and investment of tax increases on the one hand and increased prosperity among low-income people on the other, and here too, empirical opportunities are widely available. Other studies are needed on how scarce resources would and could be allocated in a more equal economy, the ultimate aim of such research being to estimate how far inequality can be reduced before negative consequences develop both for the general welfare and for the welfare of those sectors of the population who would be important political supporters or opponents of more equality.

All of these possible studies are also examples of one much larger study, on the functions that inequality now serves for society as a whole, or at least for particular sectors of it. If inequality is necessary to maintain a society with a complex division of labor and a high standard of living for at least some, then the extent to which it is necessary ought to be specified in detail, to determine the eventual likelihood of more equality, the functional alternatives that would have to be developed for existing functions that are socially or politically necessary, and the amount of reduction in inequality that the society, economy, and polity can tolerate before the dysfunctions of that reduction begin to overwhelm its functions.

Yet perhaps the most perplexing problems arise with respect to political equality, and research is needed on its possibilities and problems, and on the politics of equality as well. For one thing, political theorists need to rework the theory of democracy in an egalitarian direction, replicating what John Rawls has done for legal theory. Can democracy, which originated as an elite method of governance, be transformed into an egalitarian method, and if so, with what consequences for the polity? It is not difficult to propose measures for making the vote egalitarian, but voting is only one, and that a minor, part of the political process, and imaginative social invention is needed to design a more egalitarian but still workable federal executive and legislature, not to mention more egalitarian bureaucracies. More important yet is the democratization of economic power, and the invention and testing of an egalitarian corporation that incorporates not only worker control but also customer control. Similarly, it is not difficult to imagine greater political participation, but aside from the empirical question whether people are willing to participate more, there are such questions as whether decisions can still be reached in any polity that is heterogeneous, participatory, and egalitarian, and to what extent fuller participation—and more egalitarian politics in general— would simply give greater power to the majority and repress minorities and their demands. Moreover, libertarians have criticized egalitarian proposals because they enlarge the scope and power of government, and while they have been mainly concerned that bigger government would deprive them of their privileges, the question remains whether it is possible to envisage a government that would not seek to maximize its own power and resources even if it equalized liberty among greater numbers of its constituents. Institutions with a monopoly in their realm are never inclined to be egalitarian if they are free not to be, and some "de-monopolization" of government would be necessary, or at least the invention of a new checks-and-balances system that would operate *on* government rather than within it.[4]

For political and other social scientists interested in more empirically grounded problems, the politics of equality is a ripe subject. Historically inclined researchers could go back into the American past to discover what egalitarian legislation exists and why it became law; they could also look into the much larger number of egalitarian proposals that failed of passage. For example, the legislative and political history of the federal income tax should be explored from an egalitarian perspective, to discover how and why a mildly progressive tax was passed at the beginning of the twentieth century and what has happened since; why progressive state income taxes have been approved by the voters in some states and not in others; and why social security did not become a progressive tax. Then there is the more general question why egalitarian thought and egalitarian movements have been so scarce in America, even among socialists.

Such studies can also be carried forward to our time, to find out why the poor, the working class, and even the moderate-income population, all of whom would gain from egalitarian legislation, are not resorting to more political action, which raises the more general question why, despite the priority economic interests have in the political process, most people often seem unwilling or unable to pursue their economic interests through politics. In this connection, one must also look at the high degree of formal political decentralization that exists in America, and thus to ask whether it—together with the tendencies toward economic, administrative, and informal political centralization that seem to mark the postindustrial segments of American society at least—hinder and perhaps even emasculate any grass-roots egalitarian political impulses. In addition, there is the question what role the nature of American society, particularly that of its seemingly open class structure, plays in the scarcity—at least so far—of egalitarian political movements and egalitarian politics in America; and in line with the observations in Part I of this book, whether such phenomena as the decline of economic growth and the increasing centralization of economic and political power may not only "close" that class structure in the years to come, but bring with it some of the political manifestations of such a class structure that have long been seen in Europe, and in developing countries emerging from colonialism and tribal autocracy.

In fact, considerable light can be shed on the American experience and on the possibilities for more equality in the future by looking at other countries, particularly those which have been pursuing egalitarian policies of various kinds. Almost all of the Western European countries have pursued such policies in recent years, and so have the Eastern European ones, as well as the People's Republic of China, Cuba, and other Asian, African, and Western Hemisphere nations. Not only are their current policies in income redistribution and maintenance, job creation and democratization, worth examining, but historical studies ought to be made as well, to discover how and why such policies came into being.

Cross-national comparative studies are extremely useful in providing examples of new policy ideas, especially those which have worked, as long as one does not assume that the experience of other nations can be imported directly into America. The European welfare states that have achieved more progressive tax, transfer payment, and employment programs differ from America in their politics and their class structure, and programs that work in an ethnically homogeneous and more openly stratified society with a highly centralized and not always very representative democratic polity may not work in America. The experience of socialist and communist countries is further removed from American conditions, in which a socialist revolution is highly unlikely, but even so, many of these countries achieved some degree of income redistribution after the revolutionary takeover and brought it about by nonviolent means and without the large-scale expropriation and killing of the affluent that marked early Russian and Chinese policy.

Finally, egalitarian research ought to pay attention to some of the critical analyses of egalitarian policies that have been made by conservative social scientists, for whatever their value position, the writings of such conservatives as Milton Friedman are characterized by a tough-minded realism that egalitarian research would do well to copy. The main contribution of conservative writers is to show that innovation, especially in the form of government social policy, will either not work or will be accompanied by unintended but undesirable consequences, and their pessimistic analyses ought to be examined and tested, for they provide ideas about consequences which egalitarian researchers might otherwise ignore. Similarly, attention should be paid to the work of radical social scientists, for even though they tend to evaluate all social phenomena in terms of whether or not they advance the revolutionary cause, and often make overblown claims about the ripeness of society for revolutionary change, they are also more

aware of systemic contradictions and of the faults of proposals for evolutionary change than social scientists of a
liberal or left-liberal bent.

NOTES

This essay was written especially for this volume. Another version of
Chapters Seven and Eight was presented as the presidential address
at the 1973 meeting of the Eastern Sociological Society.

1. See particularly Melvin M. Tumin, "On Inequality," *American
   Sociological Review*, vol. 28 (February 1963), pp. 19–26, and his
   earlier articles in the debate with Davis and Moore, "Some Principles of Stratification: A Critical Analysis" and "Reply to Kingsley Davis," in Reinhard Bendix and Seymour M. Lipset, eds.,
   Class, Status and Power, 2nd ed. (New York: Free Press, 1966),
   pp. 53–8, 62–4.
2. See, e.g., Eva Rosenfeld, "Social Stratification in a Classless
   Society," *American Sociological Review*, vol. 16 (December 1951),
   pp. 766–74; Richard D. Schwartz, "Functional Alternatives to
   Inequality," *American Sociological Review*, vol. 20 (August 1955),
   pp. 424–30; Amitai Etzioni, "Functional Differentiation of Elites in
   the Kibbutz," *American Journal of Sociology*, vol. 64 (March 1959),
   pp. 476–87; Melvin Spiro, *Kibbutz*, 2nd ed. (New York: Schocken
   Books, 1970); Bruno Bettelheim, *Children of the Dream* (New
   York: Macmillan Co. 1969); the many articles by the late Yonina
   Talmon, and Yonina Talmon, *Family and Community in the
   Kibbutz* (Cambridge, Mass.: Harvard University Press, 1972). The
   literature on egalitarian policies in Communist countries is too
   vast to cite here.
3. See, e.g., Rosabeth M. Kanter, *Commitment and Community*
   (Cambridge, Mass.: Harvard University Press, 1972); Benjamin
   Zablocki, *The Joyful Community* (Baltimore: Penguin Books,
   1971); Bennett M. Berger *et. al.*, "Child-Rearing Practices of the
   Communal Family," in Arlene S. and Jerome H. Skolnick, eds.,
   Family in Transition (Boston: Little, Brown & Co., 1972), pp.
   509–23; and Kathleen Kinkade, *A Walden Two Experiment* (New
   York: William Morrow & Co., 1973).
4. These observations are all instances of the possibilities and prob-
   lems of societal guidance raised by Amitai Etzioni, *The Active
   Society* (New York: Free Press, 1968).

8
Some Utopian Scenarios

Complete equality is a utopian idea, but utopian ideas are worth exploring to suggest future directions for existing society. This chapter presents a number of utopian scenarios, brief speculative sketches of hypothetical societies, each designed around a different kind of complete equality. The scenarios emphasize some of the consequences that would follow and the problems that would have to be solved under complete equality, because they are also intended to shed some light on the consequences and problems of policies for more equality.

Scenario is a popular term approximating what social scientists call models or simulations, and model-building is common practice today in a number of social sciences. These models attempt to simulate existing societies, whereas utopian models must be speculative. Even though they should be grounded in current theoretical insights and empirical knowledge about the workings of existing societies, they have to depend heavily on thoughtful guessing about how institutions and people might behave under radically different circumstances, thus moving far beyond whatever is scientific in social science. Nevertheless, I think such "research" is useful for the social sciences, because it requires the application of informed imagination to the study of society, which not only might encourage researchers to realize the relationist quality, to use Karl Mannheim's concept, of current social arrangements, but would also generate many new research questions about how existing society operates.

Properly speaking, utopian models should include three components: the *definition* of the egalitarian condition; the social, economic, and other *prerequisites* necessary to a society before such equality can exist; and the various *consequences* for other parts of the society that accompany the kind of equality under discussion. The scenarios I am presenting here do not measure up to this standard; some ignore prerequisites entirely and others emphasize them at the expense of consequences. Moreover, all are brief and exceedingly simple in conception and scope; they are only preliminary illustrations of scenarios that ought to be constructed rather than finished products.

Finally, the scenarios are only partially utopian; in fact, they begin with the nonutopian premise that people in these hypothetical societies would pursue their self-interest as they do in existing ones. I set up this premise partly because I do not believe that utopias which assume a very different "human nature" are useful, and partly because one of my purposes in writing the scenarios was to discover the conflicts between complete equality and self-interest. The scenarios are only partially utopian in other ways as well, for I have tended to assume the presence of some existing institutions, referring, for example, to corporations in an economically egalitarian society. This is in part intentional, for I assume that a large society will require corporations of some kind even if it is egalitarian, but this also reflects the primitive and incomplete design of my scenarios, for I have obviously not thought about what kind of economic organization is most congruent with equality.

The scenarios included here discuss economic, political, racial, sexual and familial, educational, and cultural equality. One major omission is class equality, since I find it difficult to imagine a classless society, at least with the size, complexity, and standard of living of a modern society.

Economic Equality

By economic equality, I mean here equality of income and wealth, leaving out equality of occupational status or equality in the workplace. For brevity's sake, I shall limit the scenario to one kind of income equality, in which everyone earns about the median income, thus leaving out such alternatives as the *kibbutz* in which economic equality is achieved by the communal provision of all goods and services and no one receives personal income, except for pocket money and vacation allowances; the socialist models involving public ownership of the economy; and the so-called Cuban model in which the state hopes to supply all basics such as bread and milk, shelter, medical services, and transportation for nothing, but continues wage and salary differentials.

There are even a number of median-income models, each with different social implications. One provides for wage and salary equality, which would probably make it difficult to recruit workers for onerous jobs and would require other rewards to demarcate status differences. Another, which I shall choose, maintains wage differentials, using the tax system to create equality. Even within this model, further distinctions must be made, based on the time period and the social unit for which equality is computed. Thus, incomes could be equalized every year, every nth year, or over a person's lifetime. In the latter case, people could draw most heavily on their lifetime income at the time they need it most, for example, while raising their families.

The social unit can be, among others, the household (assuming here it is equivalent to the nuclear family), or adult individuals (although one could also conceive of a model in which children obtained full income equality as well). Each of these would have different social consequences; with the household as the unit, present family arrangements would probably continue, at least if additional allowances were made for children, although children would be encouraged to set up new households more quickly, so that both the family of origin and that of procreation would be able to maximize their family income. If no extra money were allocated for children, fertility and family size might well decline, since some people would prefer to spend their limited income on other things; if allowances for children were included, some families might have more children than today, particularly since they would not be able to earn additional after-tax income through work or investment. However, if the allowances were set strictly in terms of the cost of raising children at different ages, so that they would not provide additional family income, fertility would not be affected. If individuals were the social unit, then people earning above the median might decide not to marry, though as long as two people could live more cheaply than one, the incentive not to marry would be slight. More important, people establish families mainly for noneconomic reasons, so that different egalitarian policies probably would have only a minor impact on family formation and size.

The economic-equality scenario developed here will assume the retention of wage differentials, with equality achieved annually or more often through the tax system, enabling all adult individuals to have equal incomes, with cost-level allowances for children determined both by their number and their age. Under such a scheme, women would obtain more equality than they have now, since after-tax family income would be the same whether they or their husbands worked, but they could also remain housewives, and family size would not ride on economic considerations.

Insofar as economic equality extended to wealth, families would no longer be able to pass their wealth on to the next generation and thus to perpetuate themselves as dynasties. In fact, unless some people had the power to send their children to the best schools, they could not pass on much of their own status, and if economic equality reduced incentives for education, as I suggest subsequently, then even less so. The extent to which the generational transmission of economic and social resources is important to family cohesion and structure is hard to estimate, but if it is important, parents would oppose any egalitarian scheme that prohibited it, and if it were instituted, some might not want to have children at all. If it is not important, then parents might take less interest in their children when they became adolescent, for if their children could not guarantee them immortality, they might have less need to shape their lives along parental lines. On the one hand, this might free adolescents from adult domination; on the other, it might increase the social distance between the two age groups once their life-styles diverged. Younger children, however, would continue to be dependent on parents, and parents would thus have more incentive to shape them according to parental culture. In fact, they might exert more pressure on young children to be like themselves, knowing that they could not exert this pressure in adolescence. (This is the case among many working-class and poor families in our society, and it may be related to the fact that they have few resources to pass on to their children.)

Needless to say, an economically equal society would be very different in other respects from the present one, for poverty and great affluence—and all the pathology, problems, and conflict they generate—would be eliminated. If this scheme were implemented now, a family of four would have an annual income between $15,000 and $20,000, plus their share of the redistributed wealth, and assuming no major change in price levels, everyone would be comfortably off if not affluent. But assuming also that the normal human desire for more income would continue, people would try to obtain further income in various ways. As I noted in Chapter Three, suburban gardens would be planted with vegetables so as to allow expenditure of money income for other goods, people would exchange certain types of labor with each other, and barter of various kinds could be expected as well. People working in consumer-goods industries and stores would probably try to take home more of their employers' products than they do now, and firms that wanted to attract skilled workers when the supply was scarce would no doubt offer a variety of fringe benefits that added to real income, such as automobiles that could be used off the job and sales or other conferences at vacation resorts. Consequently, tax regulations would have to control such benefits so that they did not create excessive new inequalities. Individuals who could not restrain their need for more income might turn to bank robbery for this purpose, although their number would probably be small, for a society willing to establish economic equality would have various formal and informal ways of discouraging greed.

People would continue to work for noneconomic reasons alone—though surely not as hard—but since higher wages would bring them only more status and not more spending power, they would reject onerous jobs and flood the market for more desirable ones, thus forcing society to provide other incentives and sanctions to make sure the onerous work got done and supply-demand equilibrium was established for the more desirable jobs. Onerous jobs could be filled by reducing the number of work hours, but it is not clear whether corporations could be run by twenty-hour-a-week executives, or whether firms could operate with any degree of efficiency with employees working different numbers of hours. Moreover, the people with shorter work periods would have more time to grow vegetables or produce goods for barter. Symbolic rewards such as national honors might recruit some people for some jobs, but another solution would be to rotate desirable and undesirable jobs, as is done in the *kibbutz*. This is more difficult in a large society than in a community-sized one, and would reduce efficiency and productivity when well-trained people were lost by rotation. Of course, people could be allowed to work longer hours without additional recompense, and those who especially enjoyed their work might do so, but then they would shrink the supply of desirable jobs. Perhaps a better solution is the "industrial army" proposed by Edward Bellamy in *Looking Backward,* in which every member of society was required to put in a period of years at the most onerous jobs before being free to look for work of his or her choice. Nevertheless, some necessary jobs might not be taken, and some people might have to be paid more to fill needed roles. If their number was small and they could not pass their higher incomes on to their children, such a deviation from complete equality would probably not be problematic, although if the deviants could also obtain more political power, the seeds of a new elite would have been sown.

With income equality, there would be little incentive to save and investment would have to become a public function, creating political problems to be discussed below. The market mechanism could probably determine investment for consumer goods and services, and costly personal services, such as medical care, could be provided publicly on the basis of need, but other public investment decisions are difficult to make on an egalitarian basis, since they often benefit some people more than others. For example, if income equality did away with private philanthropists who now subsidize expensive high culture and the government had to invest in the production of chamber music concerts, the few people attending such concerts would obtain high per capita benefits at the expense of the rest of the population. An egalitarian society might decide that such concerts would have to be abolished as one price of equality, and chamber music would be available only on records, or in private concerts given in people's living rooms.

If work ceases to be a source of higher income, educational motives will change. Some people will then decide to pursue the liberal-arts education educators have always dreamed of, and those with shorter work weeks may go to school to keep busy, but many others will decide that education is unnecessary or unenjoyable, and a mechanism will have to be invented to make sure that the jobs requiring a great deal of prior education are filled. Most likely, the needed skills could be imparted through more on-the-job training, but the jobs that require intensive schooling could be filled only by paying people their full income for and while going to school. Society could of course provide everyone with a free college education, and even make it compulsory so as to postpone a rush on the labor market, but this would penalize students who did not want such an education and the teachers who would have to teach them; and if universities became in effect places that provided training for potential workers, they would be far more vocational than they are today.

Income equality would result in a radical change in the class structure, although wage differentials and the division of labor would maintain some kind of social differentiation and stratification. People holding the hardest-to-fill jobs would have the highest status, and if they were able to withhold their labor by striking, they would presumably have more political power than the rest of the population. Consequently, such a society would have to make sure that hard-to-fill jobs were kept at a minimum by job redefinition and work rationalization. Similarly, executives and others who have power over workers or whose decisions affect the economy and the society would still have more status, and would join the scarce workers at the top of the socio-economic hierarchy, but their power to generate new inequality for themselves could be discouraged at least to some extent by job rotation, and by making them elected officials whose decisions were regulated by a constituency of workers and others. This would undoubtedly affect efficiency and productivity in some cases, but an egalitarian society would have to reconcile itself to such effects.

For the majority of people, status differences would no longer be determined by income or work, and new sources of differentiation would develop. For example, if people no longer clustered socially or residentially on the basis of income, they might do so by age, ethnic origin, religion, kind of education, and leisure interests. If reduction of work hours became the major incentive to fill needed jobs, the people working the fewest hours would not only have the most status but would be sure to congregate socially and residentially, since a life-style based on a twenty-hour work week would be quite different from one based on a work week of thirty to thirty-five hours, and people with a lot of free time would associate with each other to develop common ways of spending that free time. The ways in which people chose their neighbors and communities would thus change drastically.

Moreover, with income equality, money would be too scarce to justify the building of large houses as indicators of status; except for the few who wanted to spend extra amounts of money or their own labor for distinctive housing, most people would live in much more uniform dwellings than now. In fact, housing would be designed more to fit age and family-size needs, since people could save money by buying less housing space when they were single or old, which would in turn encourage further current trends of residential clustering by position in the life-cycle.

If community and housing choices were no longer made on the basis of present class and status considerations, many people would become more mobile. A Boston Brahmin might stay in his home town because, even with a lower income, he would still derive some status from his historic family background and his connections, but more people than ever would head for warmer and pleasanter climates, particularly to regions where they could live with lower heating bills and grow more of their own food. In fact, family farming might undergo a small renaissance.

With income differences eliminated by taxation, politics would cease to be a conflict between the haves and

the have-nots, although traditional political differences—
for example, between producers and consumers, landlords
and tenants, or urban and rural residents—would persist.
New ones would develop as well; for example, if people
congregated in terms of interests, communities of sports
enthusiasts would fight with communities of hobbyists over
public investments for their respective leisure pursuits, and
within the former, golfers would fight with hikers about
whether open space should be devoted to golf courses or
wilderness areas. People who worked full-time would ask
government to prevent those with more spare time from
earning extra income by producing goods for barter, or
to grant them public benefits that would add an equivalent
amount to their own incomes. And since full-time workers
would constitute a political majority, they would have the
power to achieve their demands, at least if democracy
means majority rule. People who are politically powerful
by virtue of high positions in the economy would also
attempt to get extra benefits, although if their numbers
were small and if politicians did not depend on them or
their companies for campaign funds, their political power
would be much less than it is today. But perhaps the major
political struggles would be over public investment, with
all groups trying to pressure government for decisions that
would mean extra benefits for them, and here too, their
numerical power as well as their organizational skill would
determine to what extent public decisions were deflected
from egalitarian principles.

In order to maintain economic equality, the best solution for government would be to transfer as many of its
regulatory powers to bureaucracies that did not need to
respond to the electorate, but this would make the society
less democratic and the bureaucracies too powerful. Indeed, unless all citizens accepted the desirability of economic equality, a conflict might soon arise between

egalitarian and democratic principles. But even if this did not happen, government itself would have to proliferate, since it would be saddled with the responsibility of keeping the economy egalitarian. Although such proliferation is less dangerous than today's opponents of equality suggest, and, if government is democratic, less dangerous than the proliferation of corporations large enough to free themselves from control by customers, investors, or political regulators, it does put more power into the hands of a monopolistic institution, and monopoly power is dangerous for equality whether in private or in public hands.

It is possible, of course, to argue that the benefits of economic equality, particularly for the population that now earns less than the median, outweigh any of these costs, but such costs are inevitable, and who is to bear them is itself a major political issue. Once-poor people might well favor a government that obtained a median income for them, even if government officials lived better than they, but people who had to give up some income would not share their opinion, and intellectuals would suffer if government were powerful enough to restrict criticism and civil liberties. Whether it is possible to create political and bureaucratic mechanisms that would enable government to protect equality without accruing unequal powers and privileges is perhaps one of the most important unanswered questions in designing an economically egalitarian scenario.

POLITICAL EQUALITY

A politically egalitarian scenario is much harder to describe than an economically egalitarian one, for as I noted before, power is less easily divided than money, and any large society with a division of labor requires some delegation of authority, which can result in inequality. In fact, complete political equality probably requires the breakup of the nation-state, for if people were to have equal amounts of power in determining their fate, they would have to live in small communities with direct democracy, or at least a low degree of representative democracy. Moreover, such communities would have to be fairly homogeneous in population, for direct democracy can work only when it is grounded on a considerable degree of consensus, and with heterogeneity, majorities could create inequality for minorities. Smallness and homogeneity go together, for only a small community can develop the cohesion that will motivate people to give up benefits for the sake of others, for example, to allow children to train themselves for jobs not needed by the community, which with respect to artists and scientists has been a problem even in the relatively homogeneous *kibbutz*. Such communities would either have to be so poor that the mere struggle for survival made the community's well-being every person's self-interest, or so affluent that no one had scarce resources or skills the control of which could become a source of extra power.

In addition, politically egalitarian communities would need to be economically self-sufficient, for they cannot long maintain political equality if they become involved in relationships with other communities, unless these are also egalitarian. For example, if a community had to earn part of its living by trading with other communities, then those people and firms carrying out the trade would obtain a degree of economic power that would soon translate itself into political power, although this might be ameliorated if the economic enterprises of the community were publicly owned. Consequently, complete political equality would probably be best achieved by farming communities that could feed themselves, but the attainment of such equality would mean a lower standard of living for everyone—provided of course that the individual communities would refrain from making war on each other to enrich themselves.

Whether or not people would partake of the opportunity for political equality in small communities is another question. The *kibbutz* experience suggests that people would participate in issues critical to the survival of the community and issues in which they were personally interested, leaving the rest of the decision-making to elected representatives or to self-selected individuals who enjoy politics. Given the smallness of the community, access to and control over such representatives would be easy, so that they would always have a good sense of what their constituents wanted or would accept and would not be likely to disobey the general will when it manifested itself.

In a large, heterogeneous nation-state, complete political equality is probably unattainable, but scenarios for maximizing it can be suggested. For this purpose, it is useful to distinguish between equality of participation, equality of access to political representatives, and equality of control over them. Equality of participation begins with the right of one person to have one vote and to have the opportunity to vote more often than at biennial and quadriennial elections. Voting could be equalized simply by creating election districts of roughly equal size, instituting proportional representation, and funding election campaigns with federal monies. However, voting is only one kind of participation, and not a very effective one at that, for it is available only infrequently and gives voters little choice except between rival candidates.

The most effective form of participation is the exertion of political pressure, but this is difficult to equalize.

It might be possible to equalize the *ability* to exert pressure, which would probably require economic and educational equality for all citizens, as well as methods of encouraging and giving added weight to pressure from unorganized citizens and of discouraging and discounting that of organized groups. Even if this were feasible, the *willingness* to exert pressure would also have to be equalized, and this is far more difficult, for it is a function of individual and group needs. People who wanted something from government or were dissatisfied with its performance would be willing to engage in pressure activities, thus gaining a political advantage over people who wanted nothing or were satisfied. Consequently, a politically egalitarian society would probably have to minimize the opportunity for pressure politics, emphasizing instead elections and other forms of feedback in which everyone not only could but had to participate.

Involuntary participation could be created by frequent elections and referenda. Modern communications technology even makes it possible to design a feedback system by which people voice their opinions once a month or even once a week, either by telephone or by a device attached to the television set.[1] This of course assumes that everyone has access to a telephone or television set and is available to "cast" an opinion at the required time. An alternative approach is to establish a national opinion poll which interviews a sample of citizens frequently and regularly to get their reactions to current issues and upcoming decisions, with the sample large enough to narrow the amount of error and make sure that the entire opinion spectrum is adequately represented for statistical and political purposes.

Whatever the scheme, public opinion would thus provide more feedback to government, provided of course that government was required to take it into account. Even so, a number of problems would have to be dealt with. First and most important, insofar as a vote or opinion is affected by the nature of the ballot or the poller's questions, the people who made up the ballot or the questions would have the power to shape the feedback. The power of the news media would also be enhanced, for most people get from them the information on which to base their vote or opinion. However, unless the right to frame voting alternatives and poll questions was itself democratically determined, and news about all alternatives was widely disseminated, a feedback scheme would not provide greater political equality, and could easily become a mockery of the democratic process, as it often has in dictatorships that conduct carefully supervised elections and referenda. Second, a feedback scheme can only work if everyone is required to vote, for if voting or participating in a poll is voluntary, people may not express themselves on issues that do not interest them, and a minority of the population or an interest group mounting a campaign to arouse its constituents can thus swing the "election." Third, any feedback results that are evaluated by majority rule will mean less equality for the "losers." In a society where government plays a minor role, this is not very important, but in an egalitarian society, government plays a major role and many phases of social life will automatically be politicized, so that devices for guaranteeing the representation and rights of numerical minorities must be provided.[2]

If government decisions were required to follow the results of these feedback schemes, people would have not only more equality of participation but also more equality of access. Still, such access would be indirect, and if political pressure was to be discouraged, direct access would have to be also. Assuming for the moment that ways could

be found to allow direct access without its leading to unequal pressure politics, such access could be equalized only
to a limited extent. In a large society, it is obviously impossible to give every citizen equal access to his or her
political representative, for no representative will have time
to see everybody.[3] Access could be equalized by reducing
the size of political units, for example, if congressional
districts were reduced to one-fifth or one-tenth of their
present size; but this would require a much larger Congress,
thus reducing even further the already small amount of
power of an individual representative. Moreover, giving
every citizen equal access to a representative might not
properly equalize access, for an individual citizen would
then have more access than one who represented others, for
example, an organizational leader or a company president.
Insofar as such people are themselves properly elected
representatives of other citizens, they deserve more access
than the individual who speaks only for himself or herself.

Equal access does not guarantee equal control, however, for even if everyone could make contact with his or
her representative, that representative could not grant all
wishes equally without bankrupting the public treasury or
acceding to contradictory demands. In a large, heterogeneous society, a political representative must therefore
be free to decide whose demands will be granted, thus
automatically reducing the equality of those whose demands are rejected. Some correction of this result is possible by making sure that at least all major interest groups
obtain access and control, so as to correct the present situation in which affluent and organized interest groups can
"buy" a congressman or senator but less affluent and less
organized interest groups cannot. Under completely egalitarian conditions, all interest groups should have their own
representative, which would also require an enlargement

of the Congress. A yet more difficult problem stems from the fact that every person "belongs" to a number of interest groups because of the multiplicity of roles that exists in modern society, and a completely egalitarian polity requires a political system where all such roles have access and control, so that an individual would be represented as a worker, parent, church member, hobbyist, and so on. In theory, it might be possible to design a political system with several legislatures, each concerned with a specific role, but ultimately, a central legislature and executive would have to establish priorities among roles and make final decisions.

Another approach to equalizing control is to reduce the differences between the citizen and the politician, and one way of doing this is by lot, or by random selection of the latter from among the former. If all citizens are equally capable of exercising their democratic rights, then presumably they are also equally capable of representing other citizens and could therefore be assigned to political office from the population by random selection. Thus citizens would be put directly in control, although in a heterogeneous society the political results would not be much different from electing professional politicians, since the randomly chosen citizens would have to act much the same way, given the heterogeneity of their constituencies. If anything, they might be less effective at dealing with their role or their constituents until they had learned the ropes. Nonprofessional politicians now are elected to office in small towns and suburbs and, though politician enough to stand for election, are amateurs at the start, but ultimately their behavior is much the same as that of professionals.

As for the consequences of political equality, an egalitarian polity would find it more difficult to make decisions, for once more people obtained political access and control, more alternatives and interests have to be considered—and placated—and often politicians would find it impossible to make decisions, or would make them only by setting their constituencies against each other so as to give themselves more freedom to maneuver. In fact, an egalitarian polity can probably work only if society is more homogeneous than it is today, and if fewer conflicts and contradictions have to be dealt with in reaching decisions. Consequently, political equality would have to be preceded by economic equality, thus eliminating one major source of heterogeneity and contradiction. Conversely, political equality would itself encourage more economic equality, insofar as poorer citizens would be able to put pressure on government for income and other forms of redistribution, and the affluent would have lost much of the political power that now enables them to prevent economic equality.

The nature and extent of political participation would depend on whether the polity had to require involuntary participation and discourage pressure in order to remain egalitarian. If the freedom to exert pressure could be preserved, individuals and groups with demands or dissatisfactions would obviously participate more than the rest of the population, as in existing societies. If participation had to be limited to involuntary feedback, people with intensely felt demands and dissatisfactions would be restricted to private grumbling, although it is hard to imagine that such grumbling would not become a form of feedback if it was widespread.

Insofar as involuntary participation provided everyone the feeling of having a voice in the governance of society, trust in government should be higher than in existing societies, at least among people whose opinions coincided with government decisions. If popular feedback was combined with majority rule, however, the people whose opinions frequently place them in the minority might quickly lose faith in the democratic character of the feedback machinery, and in the responsiveness of government as well. Public trust would therefore depend to a considerable extent on the ability of government to take minority opinions into account and to reconcile conflicting demands. In fact, the people whose opinions were powerless and whose demands were unsatisfied might come to believe that political equality which did not benefit them was a sham, and they might become even more distrustful of government than in existing and unequal societies. Moreover, because society would be completely politicized and almost every matter would wind up before the politicians, everyday life would become more disputatious—and newspapers and television news programs longer. If trust in government's ability to deal with conflicting political demands evaporated, the society might well become highly polarized, and in a crisis, a demagogue who promised simple solutions to complex questions might obtain considerable support, at least for a while. Whereas an egalitarian polity could realize the fondest expectations of democratic theory, it would also raise popular expectations for governmental performance, and when high expectations could not be met, such a polity might be quite fragile.

Finally, the recruitment of politicians would probably change; as more people became part of the political process, they would support politicians more like themselves, and the demographic make-up of Congress would be more similar to that of the total population than at present. Politicians would have to be more astute—and perhaps more manipulative—in order to cope with the greater amount of feedback and access, and they would not have time to be technical experts on any of the issues with which they have to deal. Consequently, politicians would have to rely more on assistants who were technical experts; but expertise would be highly politicized, and much more knowledge would be needed about the effects of various decisions for specific goals and values so that the technical experts could give the right kind of political advice to the politicians for whom they worked.

RACIAL EQUALITY

Racial equality requires that people be treated as equals with respect to their racial characteristics and culture, and that race be eliminated as a distinguishing criterion in society with respect to everything else, for as I suggested in Chapter Three, race does not affect social functioning and performance. A racially equal society would thus be one in which racially based identities, subgroupings, and even cultures might continue to exist, but in which people of one race would have equality of results in terms of income, political power, and so forth with the rest of the population, and median income for one race would be the same as for another.

In a racially equal America where 15 percent of the population was black, about 15 percent of the politicians, executives, professors, electricians, and laborers would also be black, as would 15 percent of the alcoholics and drug addicts and mentally ill. Such a society would require a drastic economic and political upgrading of the current black population, but after this was achieved, blackness would no longer be a significant criterion of social differentiation. If slums continued to exist, about 15 percent of the slum dwellers would be black, but 85 percent would be white, and most people would no longer associate slum dwelling with blackness. Indeed, color would cease to be a covert indicator of social class, and eventually color awareness would decline, resulting finally in the elimination of all racial discrimination.

Under such conditions, some blacks might continue to identify themselves as blacks, explore black history, and create black culture, but for most blacks, color differences would be of much less importance, and they would become part of the over-all population, differentiating themselves from other people by whatever nonracial criteria existed in society. Such equality would undoubtedly spur what is now called intermarriage, for if race were a meaningless criterion, then it would no longer be an obstacle to marriage. In the long run, then, the number of blacks would decline, as would the number of whites, and the number of racially mixed would increase. Still, given the small number of blacks in the total American population, most whites would not have the chance to marry blacks, so that the society would never become entirely uniform in skin color.

Sexual and Familial Equality

Sexual equality not only requires society to treat men and women as political and economic equals, but also eliminates the sexual basis of all roles—and their performance—except those related to procreation and other biological differences between the sexes. Familial equality goes one step further: it eliminates economic, political, and other differences between parents and children, at least at whatever age society decides children are old enough to acquire equal rights.

With sexual equality, women would presumably hold much the same kinds of jobs as men, at the same pay, since in a heavily automated society where machines do most of the heavy work already, there are few jobs women cannot perform.[4] Some now male-dominated jobs would have to adapt to mixed company; for example, men would have to discontinue the informal badinage that accompanies male-dominated jobs—at least until women decided they were ready to use the same kinds of profanity and sexual banter. In most jobs, however, little change would take place in job performance, for work is shaped more by the requirements of the work role than by the sex or personality of the role occupants. If men became nursery school and public school teachers, boys might find more male role-models in this period of their lives and girls fewer, but with sexual equality, the need for sex-based role-models would probably be reduced, except perhaps at the onset of sexual activity. Whether or not children need same-sex role-models other than parents is a moot question in any case. Coeducational athletic teams might not play the same kind of sports by the same rules, since women would presumably never be as powerful hitters in baseball and tackles in football, and new sports calling for less brute physical strength would undoubtedly be invented. New theology and cosmology would also have to be invented, for in a sexually egalitarian society, women would not be likely to worship a male deity. Wars might change too, although modern wars are so automated that women bomber pilots would act no differently than men. Women have traditionally been more opposed to war than men, but with sexual equality, such differences might disappear. Conversely, since men would play a more important role in child-rearing, they might be more reluctant to send their children off to war. Of course, as long as nation-states and national economies exist, the causes of war are not likely to be affected significantly by the existence of sexual equality.

Whether women would enter the labor force in larger

numbers is itself uncertain; if their incomes were equal to men's, and if housekeeping was paid as well as any other job, then some and perhaps even many women might want to be housewives, at least for part of their lives. Conversely, men might want to choose this occupation too, at least in larger numbers than today. Undoubtedly, many more women would want to seek careers in the more desirable and interesting jobs, for example in the professions, and if the supply of workers exceeded the number of jobs, men and women would have to share the jobs. Under such conditions, careers might no longer be defined as full-time jobs; in some cases, husbands and wives might share one job, and both might be excused from work during part of the child-rearing period without damage to productivity, particularly with an oversupply of professional workers. Indeed, the addition of further women to the labor force might make work-sharing a necessity in other kinds of jobs.

By far the largest changes would take place in the family. With sexual equality, women would no longer need to marry for economic security, and the age of marriage would rise, since many people would wait to marry until they had children. With more women pursuing careers, more of the existing family functions would be professionalized; more families would eat in communal dining rooms and restaurants, more children would be sent to nursery schools, and some version of the children's community of the *kibbutz* might spring up, as well as group child-rearing arrangements and even group family-living patterns. More labor-saving household implements would be invented, and architects would be asked to design housing that was easier to clean and take care of than present dwellings. Conversely, if people were paid for being parents and couples worked only part-time during the early child-rearing years, life would be even more home-centered than today.

Within the family itself, the division of labor and power would presumably be determined more by the occupational success of each spouse than it is today. Unless economic equality eliminated income differences for everyone, the spouse with the better job would probably have more power in the family, or if power were to lose its present association with maleness, every family would work out its own solution depending on the personalities of the partners. This probably happens even today, although since men are automatically assumed to be household heads, it is less openly acknowledged. Presumably, people would be more likely to select mates on the basis of how they wanted to divide the labor and power in the family, although in most cases, that division would be more egalitarian than it is today. Courtship would obviously change in that women would no longer need to be as passive, and the function of the college campus as a place where middle-class women look for husbands to find economic security would end. People might find their marriage partners at work, particularly if intrafamily careers were encouraged.

Some of the most interesting consequences might manifest themselves in child-rearing patterns and their results. If sexual roles became more equal and women had the same occupational and other opportunities as men, fewer mothers would have to live through their children, and insofar as male homosexuality is generated by dominating mothers and weak fathers, it might decline. Personality problems would not vanish, however, particularly if intrafamilial struggles developed over questions of power and the familial division of labor.

If sexual equality were extended to familial equality, so that children had as much economic and political power in society as adults, the effects would be even more dramatic. To begin with, parents would probably opt for small families, since they would be outnumbered and made powerless by a large brood of children. Assuming that familial equality was put off until a child was old enough to be aware of its rights, for instance in early adolescence, much would depend on what kinds of equality were given to adolescents. If they had their own income and that income played a role in total family income, then they would participate fully in family decisions, and many families would have to move back to the city, or the suburbs would have to be redesigned to make them less boring for adolescents. With equality, adolescent sexual and political activity would begin earlier than it does today, and with economic equality, many adolescents would be moving out of the parental house at an earlier age. An even more comprehensive youth culture would develop, and insofar as it conflicted with adult culture, both parents and young people would find life more comfortable if adolescents lived apart.[5] How they would live is another question, but some clues could be obtained from the *kibbutz* and from young people's living arrangements on college campuses today.

If adolescents obtained the power to decide whether or not to go to school, many would stop attending, at least until the schools were redesigned with their needs in mind, in ways suggested in the next section of this chapter. A number would presumably want to go to work at an earlier age, perhaps putting school off till later, but their being in the labor market would create the need for many more jobs, and without economic miracles society would probably have to find some way of persuading them to stay out of the labor force.

If young people were incorporated into the labor force, adulthood would be hastened, but if they stayed out of it and remained in the interstitial life-cycle status that marks contemporary adolescence, they might have a drastic impact on politics. Today, adolescents tend to be the carriers and transmitters of a society's unachieved ideals, and if adolescents had some political power, politicians would be faced with greater pressure to implement these ideals.

EDUCATIONAL EQUALITY AMONG TEACHERS AND STUDENTS

Although it is possible and useful to describe a society with educational equality, in which all citizens have the same amount and roughly the same quality of education, I have already touched on such a scenario in discussing economic equality. Consequently, I will devote this scenario to equality within educational institutions, particularly equality of control between teachers and students over the teaching process and the administration of the schools. Such educational equality would not be overly difficult to bring about; insofar as schools are run more by formal rules than by informal patterns—in contrast, say, to the family—it is in theory possible to establish schools in which students and teachers share the responsibility for school activities.

Today schools are, by and large, institutions that transmit adult knowledge and culture as interpreted by teachers and their textbooks; the students' own knowledge and culture are considered relevant mainly to extracurricular activities. An egalitarian school would presumably balance adult and student cultures, but since there are at least two kinds of student culture, two types of schools might result. One such culture is *age-specific,* the so-called youth culture adopted by children and adolescents as an age group; the other is *adult-oriented,* in the sense that it deals with the ideas and knowledge that will be relevant to young people when they become adults—as distinguished from the ideas and knowledge that adults want to perpetuate.

An age-specific school could not be an adult-run institution, and it might provide little educational equality for adults. Instead, it would become part of the more general youth culture, devoting itself mainly to the problems children and adolescents face at particular ages, including sexual, political, legal, and other problems now rarely considered part of education, as well as to the transmission and creation of contemporary youth culture. For example, high school students would no longer read *Silas Marner* or *War and Peace,* or even *Catcher in the Rye* and *Lord of the Flies,* but works by people of their own age group—and if such schools existed, book publishers would be certain to sign up youthful novelists and essayists by the dozens. In such a school, adult teachers would be almost entirely irrelevant, since they would know less about the curriculum than their students. Their role would be limited to teaching the more persistent elements of youth culture, which students, who are more likely to be interested in the currently fashionable, would otherwise largely ignore. While an age-specific school might be quite popular with students (though unpopular with teachers), another institution would then have to be created to prepare students for their adulthood, unless they obtained that preparation later through on-the-job and family-life training.

An adult-oriented school, on the other hand, would teach the skills and ideas students need as adults. What these will be is not always predictable, and adult teachers could argue that the ideas and skills they teach will be relevant in the future. Students could not dispute them with any certainty, but if they had political equality with teachers in the school, they could require the curriculum to include the ideas and skills they thought would be relevant.

The two kinds of schools I have described are ideal types; in a real situation, an egalitarian school would probably include a mixture of age-specific and adult-oriented instruction, perhaps allowing the students to dominate the former and the adults the latter. But whether the school was age-specific, adult-oriented, or both, the basic classroom routine would change, for now students and teachers would both play a role in determining what was to be taught. Teachers would no longer function as authorities but more as resource persons; their contribution would be the time, effort, and expertise in preparing educational materials and lessons once students and teachers had agreed upon what these ought to be. Still, students would also be resource persons, for on many topics they are better informed than their teachers. In that case, students would need to become part of the school's paid labor force, which on the one hand would increase the cost of education but on the other hand would provide some useful and relevant employment for the students, which would also keep them out of the adult labor market. Thus, teachers and students would sometimes share the teaching role, and with equality, students would have as much right to criticize the teachers' presentation as teachers would have to criticize the students'. In fact, an egalitarian school might free teachers to be more critical of students, for with their unilateral authority gone, presumably they would not be exposed to parental protest about the use of such authority.

The curriculum itself would have to be developed or at least supervised by a joint student-teacher group, with the individual teacher again functioning as the resource person who translates general curriculum ideas into day-to-day specifics. Presumably, student and teacher roles would here become complementary; students would stress the novel elements of the curriculum, while teachers would emphasize the more permanent aspects of adult culture, place current concerns in historical focus, and serve the more general pedagogical functions of teaching timeless skills such as reading, writing, mathematics, the scientific method, and literary analysis.

The classroom of an egalitarian school would be more lively and interesting than today's, for if students had an equal hand in the curriculum, more would be more involved in their own education. On the other hand, the teachers' role would be more complex and more difficult; they would have to relearn the student role they themselves once occupied so as to cope with criticism or questioning by students; they would have to prepare themselves more for class; and they would have the more general problem—which students would also have—of deciding whether adult or student ideas and knowledge were more applicable to a given question. Consequently, the classroom would be pervaded by more uncertainty, which has both advantages and disadvantages. Moreover, it is quite likely that teaching would have to be a young person's occupation, partly because it would be easier for young adults to accept equality with students, partly because they would be closer to student ideas and culture. Some other role would have to be found for older teachers, and they might have to shift to new jobs in mid-life, as athletes do now.

Under egalitarian conditions, students would be involved in running the school itself, and every decision made by the school—and presumably by the school system —would be a joint decision of a student-adult committee. Schools would thus become democratic institutions, with elected participation in every decision-making function. If the school were run as a conventional democracy with majority rule, students would outnumber teachers and administrators on every committee, which might put the adults into unequal positions, except that since students do not always see eye to eye, particularly in a heterogeneous student body, some groups of students might coalesce with some teachers on certain issues. For example, in a high school where working-class and lower-middle-class students outnumbered upper-middle-class ones, it is quite possible that the former would ally themselves with the teachers against the latter, particularly since bright upper-middle-class students, at least, are disliked by some teachers because of the demands they make on them. Of course, an egalitarian school system might attract different kinds of teachers with different sympathies, thus resulting in quite different political alignments. Even so, it is probably more realistic to think of decision-making groups in which students and teachers are equal in number, regardless of the student-teacher population differential.

The most difficult political problem of an egalitarian school would be over personnel policy, since teachers have to make a living from teaching, and students do not make a living from being students. Moreover, students are only temporay members of a school system, while teachers are permanent members. Consequently, some mechanism would have to be developed to provide job security to teachers without emasculating the students' role in choosing teachers, and such a mechanism is difficult to envisage. If schools had the right to extrude students on the same grounds of performance as hold for teachers, then student-teacher personnel committees would be somewhat more reluctant to fire teachers without also firing students. The student role could also become an occupational one, with students being paid for their work like anyone else

(and being fired for poor performances), a situation that
now almost prevails in graduate schools; but even so, job
loss would be a temporary phenomenon for students, while
for teachers it would mean the loss of job security as well.
These problems would be reduced considerably if schools
were homogeneous, for if students and teachers were drawn
from roughly the same socio-economic level, the basic
cultural consensus would make it easier to reconcile dis-
agreement. This would maximize equality within the
school but would also maximize inequality between
schools, since schools with more affluent populations would
provide a better education than those with less affluent
ones. If schools were integrated by class, however, equality
would be harder to achieve, for then the schools would
face the same problems as the polity, and insofar as working-class students want a different kind of education than
upper-middle-class ones, students and teachers both would
have difficulty in reconciling diverse demands. Schools have
an alternative less available to the polity: to divide the
school system up by the kinds of education that are
wanted; but then the system's ruling body would have to
make sure that all kinds of education were equally funded,
and that the more statusful or numerically dominant parts
of the system did not overpower the rest.

An egalitarian school system would also run into
trouble with the outside world, at least as long as its funds
came from taxpaying parents. Parents have generally
financed schools to prepare children for an adult-defined
adulthood, and have given teachers authority *in loco
parentis* for this purpose. Without more equality in the
family, it seems unlikely that parents would be willing to
finance an egalitarian school system over which they did
not also have some control, and in that case, parents and
teachers would frequently coalesce against the students

and end their equality. It is possible to design an economically egalitarian system in which students receive their own incomes and pay for their own education, either out of taxes or on a fee basis, but then they would be virtual employers of their own teachers, with a predictable decline in teacher equality. In that case, schools might well become more age-specific than is socially desirable, even in the students' own long-term interest, and would probably resemble student-run community centers more than schools. And if students were economically independent and school attendance was not compulsory, some students might stop going to school unless it was run as a community center. This would be particularly likely in an economically egalitarian society where people had less incentive to go to school to achieve occupational success, for then occupational training would have to take place mostly on the job in any case. In an economically unequal society, however, and particularly in one where the school was a major determinant of later occupational success, an egalitarian school system that was free of parental control might work quite effectively to produce an occupationally useful education for almost everyone, provided students and teachers were able to design the relevant curricula.

Finally, as in the case of familial equality, a decision would have to be made regarding the age at which young people are eligible for equality. In today's rapidly changing society, where the knowledge of the young is sometimes more relevant than that of adults, many adolescents are perfectly capable of assuming roles and responsibilities in an egalitarian school system, but society would still have to decide whether adolescence begins at fifteen or twelve or ten years. An economically more static society, in which adult knowledge would be more relevant and new ideas would have less power, might decide that adolescence does not begin until later. Conversely, such a society might also be interested in keeping young people out of the labor market as long as possible, and in return give them more equality in the schools.

CULTURAL EQUALITY OF TASTE LEVELS AND THE ELIMINATION OF DEVIANCE

Cultural equality is defined in two ways, even though these ways are not interrelated and are lumped together arbitrarily here. First, cultural equality means the elimination of invidious status and other distinctions between "high-brow," "middlebrow," and "lowbrow" levels of taste, or what I call high, middle, and low "taste cultures." Second, it means the elimination of all distinctions between "deviant" and "nondeviant" behavior, making the very idea of deviance irrelevant. A culturally equal society would thus treat all ways of expressing oneself and acting as equal in value, status, and moral worth. People who prefer popular music would be judged as equals of chamber music devotees; sexual, political, and other behavior patterns now punished or scorned as deviant would be as acceptable and legitimate as any others.

Taste levels are now determined largely by socio-economic status, by income, and particularly by education, for the comprehension and appreciation of high culture requires at least a college education. I have argued elsewhere that even in today's society, all taste cultures should be equal in value and cultural status, because they express the differing aesthetic standards of people in different socio-economic and educational circumstances.[6] This kind of cultural pluralism is difficult to put into practice, however, because in existing societies taste culture is evaluated by the same status criteria as other elements of life-style, and the culture of a working-class person is considered inferior to that of a rich person. Because culture is a consequence of class, cultural equality can probably be achieved only in a classless society, but then cultural equality would actually be cultural sameness.

Cultural sameness is hardly desirable, but cultural equality without too much sameness might be furthered by economic equality. While similarity of income would increase similarity of culture to some extent, it is also possible that with economic equality, people would place greater emphasis on life-styles as status symbols and as criteria for social clustering, and taste-culture differences might retain their present importance as indicators of differential status and thus as sources of inequality. Income equality might, however, reduce the status gap between high, middle, and low cultures, and the latter two would increase in status vis-à-vis the former. Although some utopians have argued that with economic equality, most people would want to become well educated and turn to "highbrow" pursuits in their spare time, just the opposite might happen. If opportunities for economic advancement were reduced, education might no longer be so important to people, and the number of those who pick up high-culture tastes along with professional skills in college might shrink. At the same time, economic equality would eliminate the philanthropists who now subsidize high culture, and that culture would either have to become economically self-sufficient or find alternative forms of subsidy. In an economically equal society in which highbrows were a small minority, such subsidies would not be likely to come from government; with any degree of political democracy, more people would want government to subsidize the construction of ski lifts and boat harbors than chamber music concerts. Writers, composers, and artists would still spring up to translate their personal drives and visions into literature, music, and art, but if high culture received fewer funds and less prestige, more might decide to work in popular cultures, and without a viable economic base, high culture would decline.

The mixture of respect and hostility with which most people view high culture would also decline under conditions of economic equality, and once its association with wealth had ended, it could more easily be treated as one culture among equals. With the status and power of high culture reduced, its critical disdain of the "lower" cultures would no longer receive as much attention, and conflict between taste cultures might decrease. In that sense, greater cultural equality would have come to pass, but mostly at the expense of high culture. Whether or not this is undesirable depends in part on one's point of view. One could argue that if the decline of high culture was one price of economic equality, the cost might well be worth the benefit. At the same time, however, high culture performs societal functions for all taste cultures, addressing itself to philosophical, aesthetic, and other issues at a level of intensity and expertise that other taste cultures do not provide and on which they themselves draw, if only in watered-down form. In fact, the distributors of popular culture might have a vested interest in maintaining—and thus subsidizing—high culture for this purpose.

In the last analysis, cultural choices are determined more by education than by anything else, and if every person received the same years of education, cultural equality would be enhanced, and while cultural sameness would increase, some differentiation would remain. For example, if every member of society received a college education and was thus prepared educationally for the pursuit of high culture, the popularity of the lower taste cultures might decline and more cultural uniformity would develop. Even so, insofar as cultural choices are determined by home backgrounds and quality differences in colleges would persist, taste differences would also remain. Moreover, the pursuit of high culture is a craft requiring an intense involvement with culture that few people are willing to undertake, so that even in a well-educated society, high-culture devotees would probably still be a minority, and upper-middle-class taste culture would be numerically supreme, with lower-middle- and working-class taste cultures declining as well. High culture would, however, increase the size of its audience as compared with today, and with political democracy, a well-educated population would want more government subsidy for it, particularly if it continued to be a source of ideas and forms for upper-middle-class culture. Conversely, the people who were unwilling or unable to go to or stay in college would become a new uncultured minority, and would undoubtedly be treated unequally.[7] Of course, if educational equality were defined as providing everyone with a median level of education (which today is about twelve years), then the most poorly and the best-educated portions of the population would disappear, and both low culture and high culture would suffer. And if society were equal both economically and educationally, the effects of income equality would probably overwhelm those of educational equality, for the incentive for education would be reduced.

Ultimately, then, cultural equality could probably come about only with the elimination of status and class differences, and only a classless society would be culturally equal. It would also be culturally more uniform, for while cultural preferences based on age, religion, and other social characteristics might remain, the reduction in the division of labor necessary for classlessness would probably eliminate professional creators of culture, high and low, and culture would be created by amateurs, as it is in most primitive societies. As such, it would probably be quite uniform.

The possibility of eliminating inequalities between deviant and nondeviant life-styles and thus of eliminating deviance would vary depending on the dominant values of the society, the societal functions of the behavior, the numbers practicing it, and on other conditions in the society. For example, victimless crime can lose its criminal character with a change in values, and if sexual values were liberalized further, prostitution might become less deviant if only because it became more superfluous. On the other hand, it is also possible that those who resorted to prostitution in a sexually liberal society would be scorned and pitied. The power and status of the "victims" of victimless crime are also a factor; the more powerful they are, the more likely that activities they do not consider criminal will not be so considered by the makers of laws.

In existing societies, deviance has an important function: to justify and uphold the normative validity of nondeviant life-styles. As long as such justification is needed, deviant life-styles must be punished or scapegoated and thus kept unequal even while they are encouraged to persist in order to perform their function. Whether a society is possible where this function of deviance is unnecessary is hard to say; economically and politically egalitarian societies would generate all kinds of new tensions that would be ameliorated, at least symptomatically, by the creation of scapegoats, and perhaps only in a society of totally unlimited resources—which is difficult to conceive —could deviance be abolished. Moreover, insofar as complete equality of any kind requires the elimination of much of the division of labor, and the decentralization of society into small homogeneous units, the need for social control mechanisms will almost certainly require the availability of deviants. For example, in a society where all work is shared equally, the persons who refuse to do their share are quickly punished or expelled.[8]

Nevertheless, the determination of deviance depends also on the numbers of people practicing it and on their status and power, so that once-deviant behaviors can assume greater legitimacy. Abortion has already begun to lose its deviant status, and in a very short time-period, probably because the women demanding it are often of high status and because abortion is also seen as a method for reducing the number of poor people. Similarly, homosexuality is no longer quite as deviant as it was, at least in some American cities. In part, this has resulted from the drifting of homosexuals to a few cities—and occupations—and from their resulting economic and political power by virtue of their numbers; but in part, the new respectability of homosexuality may also be a consequence of the lesser importance of children. In a society where people—and the economy—need many children, the homosexual is punished for not producing them; in one where children no longer serve an important economic function, such punishment is less necessary, although if the birthrate declines precipitously, homosexuality may once again become more deviant.

If this reformulation of the Durkheimian hypothesis is accurate, then the end of deviance is unlikely, and different egalitarian societies will create different deviants. In an economically egalitarian society where desirable jobs were in short supply, the person who was willing to work longer hours without compensation for the sheer joy of work might well be condemned as a rate-buster, and hoboes and others who wanted to drop out of the labor force might be encouraged. They would still be deviants, but they would no longer be punished. Some of the people who worked fewer hours and thus had to find ways of filling their leisure hours might gravitate to time-consuming lifestyles that have heretofore been considered deviant, such as above-average sexual activity and promiscuity, and if they had more status than people who worked full-time—as I suggested earlier they might have—their deviance would probably not be punished. Thus, they would be allowed some of the same liberty from cultural norms that is now permitted the rich person, the entertainer, and the celebrity. Conversely, while gambling might increase in an economically egalitarian society because it provided an opportunity to obtain extra income, it might be judged more deviant than it is today because it would violate the egalitarian ethos. Still, as long as large numbers of people wanted to add to their income by gambling, a wise egalitarian society might decide that it was the most innocuous way of enabling people to earn extra income, and it might therefore become the same publicly approved deviant behavior it is in today's America.

A politically egalitarian society might give rise to more deviance, for with more democracy, majorities would find it easier to legislate against minorities. Moreover, politicians would have considerable incentive to reduce the number of demands they must deal with, and they might thus resort to legislation that would label dissenters as deviants, much as left-wing and right-wing dictatorships are doing today.

REALISTIC EGALITARIAN SCENARIOS

Although the preceding scenarios have been unabashedly utopian, it is also possible to develop more realistic egalitarian scenarios, which work out the prerequisites and consequences of varying degrees of more equality, and ultimately, such scenarios will be more useful for egalitarian policy than utopian ones. Still, they are also harder to write, for to be useful they will have to determine the impact of a specific egalitarian proposal on existing society at a given point in time. Such specificity seems premature today, although once the political climate encourages egalitarian ideas, realistic scenarios ought to be formulated to help the policy-makers who must write the legislation and administrative guidelines for more equality.

NOTES

This essay was written especially for this volume.

1. These technologies could also be used for facilitating democratic discussion prior to polling. Experiments along this line are currently being conducted by the MINERVA project of the Center for Policy Research.
2. Some possible devices are discussed in Chapter Five.
3. Robert A. Dahl, *After the Revolution: Authority in a Good Society* (New Haven, Conn.: Yale University Press, 1970), chap. 2.
4. This section draws on Gloria Steinem, "What It Would Be Like If Women Win," *Time*, August 31, 1970, pp. 22–3.
5. For a similar idea, see Paul and Percival Goodman, *Communitas: Means of Livelihood and Ways of Life* (New York: Vintage Books, 1960), p. 147.
6. This argument is made in Herbert J. Gans, "Popular Culture in America," in Howard S. Becker, ed., *Social Problems: A Modern Approach* (New York: John Wiley & Sons, 1966), pp. 549–620; and in Herbert J. Gans, *Popular Culture and High Culture* (New York: Basic Books, forthcoming).
7. This is, of course, the premise of Michael Young's satire, *The Rise of the Meritocracy* (Baltimore: Penguin Books, 1958).
8. For an illustration, see Kathleen Kinkade, "A Walden Two Experiment," *Psychology Today*, January 1973, pp. 35–42, 90–3.

Epilogue
The Prospects
for More Equality

Theoretical and utopian discussions of equality are almost as old as organized society itself, but whatever the merits of more equality, it must also be judged by its feasibility. Thus, the relevance of this book hinges at least in part on whether the hypothesis I have propounded about the existence of an egalitarian trend in America is warranted.

Certainly there is precious little evidence in the spring of 1973 that this country is moving toward more equality and even some indication that it is now moving in the opposite direction. Some of the egalitarian movements I described, for example among students, are losing steam, and the Nixon administration is currently trying to eliminate many of the New Deal, New Frontier, and Great Society programs of the past. Not only is there little public outcry against their elimination, but the programs

235

themselves are now being described as egalitarian experiments that failed—and that should therefore be discarded forever. In fact, some observers now describe the 1960s as an aberrant decade, marked by a temporary infatuation with more equality. In reality, however, the War on Poverty and similar programs of the 1960s were hardly egalitarian, consisting mainly of traditional policies to encourage the poor to lift themselves by their own almost nonexistent bootstraps. Thus, egalitarian programs have yet to be tried, although at this writing, the political feasibility of such programs is almost nil.

Even so, it is dangerous to extrapolate too much from today's headlines, and there are some signs that the equality revolution of which I wrote is still with us. The ideas and demands associated with it continue to be voiced, and some—for example, those pertaining to more equal rights for women, racial minorities, consumers, and the victims of pollution—are now creeping into federal legislation. Another sign, albeit a terribly slender one, is the continued agitation about equality among conservative intellectuals, for evidently they were as impressed as I by what began to happen in the 1960s.

Ironically enough, even the Nixon administration policy to eliminate the old Democratic welfare programs may be a sign of the egalitarian trend, or rather, of the kind of egalitarianism that I suggested was most likely to flourish in America: for the benefit of Middle America at the expense of the poor and the racial minorities. The same policy is downgrading another group that many Middle Americans have also long viewed as a threat to their way of life: the liberal upper-middle-class professionals who invented and administered the welfare programs. And by attacking the news media and altering the structure of public television, the Nixon administration is seeking to

reduce the influence of yet other upper-middle-class professionals: those who help to create the public culture.
If these attempts succeed, we may be entering an era in
which the professional upper middle class will play a
smaller role in public policy and public culture than it has
since the days of the New Deal.

The downgrading of the professional upper middle
class will not result in more equality for Middle Americans,
however, since that class is just being replaced by a tech-
nocratic upper middle class, such as the management analysts who even now are taking over many federal agencies.
Nor are Middle Americans being favored by other Nixon
administration policies, for the current allocation of public
resources is enriching the large corporations and other
businesses that always benefit most when the Republicans
are in power. In the end, then, Middle America will only
obtain a little more symbolic equality, even while its cost
of living, its unemployment rate, and its taxes continue to
climb. The Nixonian egalitarianism is spurious, and just
the opposite of what the country needs. In fact, it is nothing more than the anti-intellectual populism that some
critics of equality falsely ascribe to egalitarian thinkers.

At the same time, the policies of the Nixon administration have not affected the basic conflict that fuels the
trend toward more equality: between the rise in popular
expectations for more autonomy, democracy, and a higher
standard of private and public living, and the continuing
centralization of the economy and the polity, with all its
implications for increasing economic and political powerlessness. As a result, I still believe that when this conflict
heightens and becomes apparent, demands that either call
for more equality or require more equality as a consequence
will begin to be voiced.

Admittedly, this prediction rests on a slim empirical

base, for in proposing a clash between higher expectations and further societal centralization, I am suggesting that *cultural* tendencies among the population will conflict with *structural* tendencies in postindustrial society, or to put it another way, that people's values will eventually drive them to oppose the social structure in which they are living.[1] And this in turn assumes that people will become more active politically in behalf of their values than they have been in the past.

Of course, the cultural tendencies and values I am describing are themselves reactions to changes in the social structure—for example, in the structure of economic opportunities for Middle Americans—and values often diverge from the behavior demanded by the social structure. Nevertheless, the question remains whether values are or can become politically significant enough forces to affect the social structure. Values are not ephemeral phenomena, but they are fragile, for they can be implemented only when people can choose between alternative forms of action, and even then, most people have so many different values that any one value is not a reliable guide as to how they will act. And when people have little choice, that is, when alternatives are sharply restricted, values are virtually irrelevant as guides to action, for then people will adapt to what they cannot change. Under such conditions, expectations will ultimately decline, and people will do as they must, holding on to their expectations only as sources of discontent to be voiced in private grumbling.

Perhaps the centralization of American society has gone so far that it cannot be changed and that people must adapt to it; and perhaps most Americans will adapt to it even if they could do otherwise, continuing to be apolitical, and looking for ways to live outside the national social structure as they have in the past, by finding satisfaction in family life, friends and neighbors, and leisure activities. Still, I suspect that as more people are directly affected by the restriction of economic and political opportunities, and as they become better educated and politically more sophisticated, a politically significant number will eventually become aware of and act on the conflict between their expectations and the structural tendencies of postindustrial society.

At that time, they will begin to exert pressure for change, but that change is likely to be uneven and slow. Diverse groups will struggle for diverse kinds and degrees of greater equality for themselves, and sometimes they will attack each other rather than the structure of society and the main holders of power, but ultimately, the economy and the polity will be bent in an egalitarian direction. The prospects for more equality are by no means certain, but they are nevertheless more encouraging than the current situation of the country would suggest.

NOTE

This essay was written especially for this volume.

1. I owe this hypothesis in part to Daniel Bell, who has also written of a forthcoming clash between culture and social structure, although he sees it as taking place between high culture and the managerial elite of postindustrial society. Daniel Bell, "The Cultural Contradictions of Capitalism," *The Public Interest*, no. 21 (Fall 1970), pp. 16–44.

A Bibliography on Equality

This bibliography includes the items relevant to equality cited in the footnotes, and a number of other books and articles which I have found useful even though they are not cited in the footnotes.

BARBER, BERNARD. *Social Stratification: A Comparative Analysis of Structure and Process.* New York: Harcourt, Brace & Co., 1957.

BARNES PETER. *The Sharing of Land and Resources in America.* Washington, D.C.: The New Republic, 1973.

BELL, DANIEL. *The Coming of Post-Industrial Society.* New York: Basic Books, 1973.

——. "Meritocracy and Equality." *The Public Interest,* no. 29 (Fall 1972), pp. 29–68.

BELLAMY, EDWARD. *Looking Backward.* New York: Lancer Books, 1968.

BERG, IVAR. *Education and Jobs: The Great Training Robbery.* New York: Praeger Publishers, 1970.

BERGER, BENNETT M., *et al.* "Child Rearing Practices of the Communal Family." In *Family in Transition,* edited by Arlene S. and Jerome H. Skolnick. Boston: Little, Brown & Co., 1972. Pp. 509–23.

BERGER, PETER. "The Arithmetic of Happiness Doesn't Add Up." *Fortune,* October 1972, pp. 151, 154.

BETTELHEIM, BRUNO. *Children of the Dream.* New York: Macmillan Co., 1969.

BLACKSTONE, WILLIAM T., ed. *The Concept of Equality.* Minneapolis: Burgess Publishing Co., 1969.

BLUMBERG, PAUL. *Industrial Democracy: The Sociology of Participation.* New York: Schocken Books, 1969.

BOWEN, IAN. *Acceptable Inequalities.* London: Allen & Unwin, 1970.

BOWLES, SAMUEL. "Getting Nowhere: Programmed Class Stagnation." *Society,* June 1972, pp. 42–9.

———, and GINTIS, HERBERT. "I.Q. in the U.S. Class Structure." *Social Policy,* vol. 3 (November 1972–February 1973), pp. 65–96.

BREAK, GEORGE. "Income Taxes and Incentives to Work." *American Economic Review,* vol. 47 (September 1957), pp. 529–49.

BRONFENBRENNER, MARTIN. *Income Distribution Theory.* Chicago: Aldine Publishing Co., 1971.

BROWN, JAMES C. *The Troika Incident.* Garden City, N.Y.: Doubleday & Co., 1970.

BUDD, EDWARD C., ed. *Inequality and Poverty.* New York: W. W. Norton & Co., 1967.

CAPLOVITZ, DAVID. *The Poor Pay More: Consumer Practices of Low Income Families.* New York: Free Press, 1962.

CARTER, ROBERT L., *et al. Equality.* New York: Pantheon Books, 1965.

CUTRIGHT, PHILLIPS. "The Distribution and Redistribution of Income." In *Power, Poverty and Urban Policy,* edited by Warner Bloomberg, Jr., and Henry Schmandt. Beverly Hills, Calif.: Sage Publications, 1968, pp. 531–64.

DAHL, ROBERT A. *After the Revolution: Authority in a Good Society.* New Haven, Conn.: Yale University Press, 1970.

DAHRENDORF, ROLF. "On the Origin of Social Inequality." In *The Concept of Equality,* edited by William T. Blackstone. Minneapolis: Burgess Publishing Company, 1969. Chap. 6.

DAVIS, KINGSLEY, and MOORE, WILBERT. "Some Principles of Stratification." *American Sociological Review,* vol. 10 (April 1945), pp. 242–9.

DE JOUVENEL, BERTRAND. *The Ethics of Redistribution.* New York: Harper & Row, 1973.

———. "The Ethics of Redistribution." In *Inequality and Poverty,* edited by Edward C. Budd. New York: W. W. Norton & Co., 1967. Pp. 6–13.

DE TOCQUEVILLE, ALEXIS. *Democracy in America.* New York: Vintage Books, 1954.

EPSTEIN, CYNTHIA, and GOODE, WILLIAM J., eds. *The Other Half: Roads to Women's Equality.* Englewood Cliffs, N.J.: Prentice-Hall, 1971.

ETZIONI, AMITAI. *The Active Society: A Theory of Societal and Political Processes.* New York: Free Press, 1968.

———. "Functional Differentiation of Elites in the Kibbutz." *American Journal of Sociology,* vol. 64 (March 1959), pp. 476–87.

FRIEDMAN, MILTON. *Capitalism and Freedom.* Chicago: University of Chicago Press, 1962.

FUCHS, VICTOR. "Redefining Poverty and Redistributing Income." *The Public Interest,* no. 8 (Summer 1967), pp. 88–95.

GALLMAN, ROBERT. "Trends in the Size and Distribution of Wealth in the 19th Century." In *Six Papers on the Size Distribution of Wealth and Income,* edited by Lee Soltow. New York: National Bureau of Economic Research and Columbia University Press, 1969. Pp. 1–25.

GANS, HERBERT J. "Equality and the Public Interest." *Journal of the American Institute of Planners,* vol. 39 (January 1973), pp. 3, 10–12.

GIL, DAVID G. *Unravelling Social Policy.* Cambridge, Mass.: Schenkman Publishing Co., 1973.

GOODE, WILLIAM J. "The Protection of the Inept." *American Sociological Review,* vol. 32 (February 1967), pp. 5–19.

GOODMAN, PAUL, and GOODMAN, PERCIVAL. *Communitas: Means of Livelihood and Ways of Life.* New York: Vintage Books, 1960.

GOODWIN, LEONARD. *Do the Poor Want to Work?* Washington, D.C.: Brookings Institution, 1972.

GROSS, BERTRAM. "A Closer Look at Income Distribution." *Social Policy,* vol. 3 (May–June 1972), p. 61.

HANSEN, W. LEE, and WEISBROD, BURTON A. "The Distribution of Costs and Direct Benefits of Public Higher Education, The Case of California." *Journal of Human Resources,* vol. 4 (1969), pp. 176–91.

HARRINGTON, MICHAEL. "Ideally, We Should Abolish Every Subsidy in the Internal Revenue Code." *Saturday Review,* October 21, 1972, p. 49.

———. *Socialism.* New York: Saturday Review Press, 1972.

HARRIS, FRED R. *Now Is the Time: A New Populist Call to Action.* New York: McGraw-Hill Book Co., 1971.

HENLE, PETER. "Exploring the Distribution of Earned Income." *Monthly Labor Review,* December 1972, pp. 16–27.

HERRIOTT, ROGER A., and MILLER, HERMAN P. "Who Paid the Taxes in 1968." Paper prepared for the National Industrial Conference Board, March 18, 1971.

JAHODA, MARIE; LAZARSFELD, PAUL; and ZEISEL, HANS. *Marienthal: The Sociography of an Unemployed Community*. Chicago: Aldine Publishing Co., 1971.

JENCKS, CHRISTOPHER, *et. al. Inequality*. New York: Basic Books, 1972.

KAHL, JOSEPH. "The Moral Economy of a Revolutionary Society." In *Cuban Communism*, edited by Irving Louis Horowitz. Chicago: Aldine Publishing Co., 1970. Pp. 95–115.

KANTER, ROSABETH M. *Commitment and Community: Communes and Utopias in Sociological Perspective*. Cambridge, Mass.: Harvard University Press, 1972.

KELSO, LOUIS, and HETTER, PATRICIA. *Two-Factory Theory: The Economics of Reality*. New York: Vintage Books, 1967.

KINKADE, KATHLEEN. *A Walden Two Experiment*. New York: William Morrow & Co., 1973.

———. "A Walden Two Experiment." *Psychology Today*, January 1973, pp. 35–42, 90–3.

KOLKO, GABRIEL. *Wealth and Power in America: An Analysis of Social Class and Income Distribution*. New York: Praeger Publishers, 1962.

KRISTOL, IRVING. "About Equality." *Commentary*, November 1972, pp. 41–7.

———. "Equality as an Ideal." In *Encyclopedia of the Social Sciences*. New York: Macmillan Co., 1968. Vol. 5, pp. 108–11.

LAMPMAN, ROBERT J. *Ends and Means of Reducing Income Poverty*. Chicago: Markham Publishing Co., 1971.

LASKI, HAROLD. "Liberty and Equality." In *The Concept of Equality*, edited by William T. Blackstone. Minneapolis: Burgess Publishing Co., 1969. Chap. 10.

LENSKI, GERHARD. *Power and Privilege: A Theory of Social Stratification*. New York: McGraw-Hill Book Co., 1966.

LIDMAN, RUSSELL. "Cost and Distributional Implications of McGovern's Minimal Income Grant Proposal." Madison: University of Wisconsin Institute for Research on Poverty, June 1972.

LUNDBERG, FERDINAND. *The Rich and the Super-Rich*. New York: Lyle Stuart, 1968.

MACAROV, DAVID. *Incentives to Work: The Effects of Unearned Income*. San Francisco: Jossey-Bass, Publishers, 1970.

McGOVERN, GEORGE. "On Taxing and Redistributing Income." *New York Review of Books*, May 4, 1972, pp. 7–11.

MARSHALL, T. H. *Citizenship and Social Class*. Cambridge: Cambridge University Press, 1950.

————. "Poverty and Inequality." Unpublished paper prepared for a project on stratification and poverty for the American Academy of Arts and Sciences, n.d.

MILLER, HERMAN P. *Rich Man, Poor Man*. New York: Thomas Y. Crowell Co., 1971.

MILLER, S. M., and RATNER, RONNIE S. "The American Resignation: The New Assault on Equality." *Social Policy*, vol. 3 (May–June 1972), pp. 5–15.

————, and ROBY, PAMELA. *The Future of Inequality*. New York: Basic Books, 1970.

MILNER, MURRAY, JR. *The Illusion of Equality: The Effects of Education on Opportunity, Inequality, and Social Conflict*. San Francisco: Jossey-Bass, Publishers, 1972.

MOYNIHAN, DANIEL P. *The Politics of a Guaranteed Income: The Nixon Administration and the Family Assistance Plan*. New York: Random House, 1973.

NEWFIELD, JACK, and GREENFIELD, JEFF. *A Populist Manifesto: The Making of a New Majority*. New York: Praeger Publishers, 1971.

PARSONS, TALCOTT. "Equality and Inequality in Modern Society." In *Social Stratification*, edited by Edward O. Laumann. Indianapolis: Bobbs-Merrill Co., 1970. Pp. 13–72.

PATEMAN, CAROLE. *Participation and Democratic Theory*. Cambridge: Cambridge University Press, 1970.

PECHMAN, JOSEPH A. "The Rich, the Poor and the Taxes They Pay." *The Public Interest*, no. 17 (Fall 1969), pp. 21–44.

————, and OKNER, BENJAMIN A. "Individual Tax Erosion by Income Classes." Paper prepared for the United States Joint Economic Committee, January 14, 1972.

PENNOCK, J. ROLAND, and CHAPMAN, JOHN W., eds. *Equality*. New York: Atherton Press, 1967.

PIVEN, FRANCES F., and CLOWARD, RICHARD A. *Regulating the Poor: The Functions of Public Relief*. New York: Pantheon Books, 1971.

PROJECTOR, D.; WEISS, G.; and THORESON, E. "Composition of Income as Shown by the Survey of Financial Characteristics of Consumers." In *Six Papers on the Size Distribution of Wealth and Income*, edited by Lee Soltow. New York: National Bureau of Economic Research and Columbia University Press, 1969. Pp. 107–56.

RAINWATER, LEE. "A Decent Standard of Living: From Subsistence to Membership." Unpublished paper, 1970.

————. *Behind Ghetto Walls: Black Family Life in a Federal Slum.* Chicago: Aldine Publishing Co., 1970.

————. "Economic Inequality and the Credit Income Tax," *Working Papers,* vol. 1 (Spring 1973). Pp. 50–61.

————. "Neutralizing the Disinherited." In *Psychological Factors in Poverty,* edited by Vernon L. Allen. Chicago: Markham Publishing Co., 1970.

————. "Public Responses to Low Income Policies: FAP and Welfare." Unpublished paper, February 1972.

————. *What Money Buys.* New York: Basic Books, forthcoming.

RAWLS, JOHN. *A Theory of Justice.* Cambridge, Mass.: Harvard University Press, 1971.

REES, JOHN. *Equality.* New York: Praeger Publishers, 1972.

ROLPH, EARL. "A Credit Income Tax." In *Poverty Policy,* edited by Theodore R. Marmon. Chicago: Aldine Publishing Co., 1971. Pp. 207–18.

ROSE, SANFORD. "The Truth About Income Inequality in the U.S." *Fortune,* December 1972, pp. 90–93, 158, 162, 167–9, 172.

ROSENFELD, EVA. "Social Stratification in a Classless Society." *American Sociological Review,* vol. 16 (December 1951), pp. 766–74.

ROSSI, ALICE K. "Sex Equality." *The Humanist,* September–October 1969, pp. 3–6, 16.

RUNCIMAN, W. G. *Relative Deprivation and Social Justice: A Study of Attitudes to Social Equality in Twentieth-Century England.* Berkeley: University of California Press, 1967.

SCHORR, ALVIN L. *Explorations in Social Policy.* New York: Basic Books, 1968.

SCHWARTZ, RICHARD D. "Functional Alternatives to Inequality." *American Sociological Review,* vol. 20 (August 1955), pp. 424–30.

SHEPPARD, HAROLD L., and HERRICK, NEAL Q. *Where Have All the Robots Gone? Worker Dissent in the Seventies.* New York: Free Press, 1972.

SKOLNICK, ARLENE S., and SKOLNICK, JEROME H., eds. *Family in Transition: Rethinking Marriage, Sexuality, Child Rearing, and Family Organization.* Boston: Little, Brown & Co., 1972.

SOLTOW, LEE., ed. *Six Papers on the Size Distribution of Wealth and Income.* New York: National Bureau of Economic Research and Columbia University Press, 1969.

SPECIAL TASK FORCE TO THE SECRETARY OF HEALTH, EDUCATION AND WELFARE. *Work in America.* Washington, D.C.: Government Printing Office, 1973.

SPIRO, MELFORD E. *Kibbutz: Venture in Utopia.* Rev. ed. New York: Schocken Books, 1970.

STEIN, BRUNO. *On Relief: The Economics of Poverty and Public Welfare.* New York: Basic Books, 1971.

STEINBERG, ALAN. "The Case for a Wealth Tax." *Social Policy,* vol. 3 (March–April 1973), pp. 51–4.

STEINEM, GLORIA. "What It Would Be Like If Women Win." *Time,* August 31, 1970, pp. 22–3.

STERN, PHILIP. *The Rape of the Taxpayer.* New York: Random House, 1973.

TALMON, YONINA. *Family and Community in the Kibbutz.* Cambridge, Mass.: Harvard University Press, 1972.

———. "Sex Role Differentiation in an Equalitarian Society." In *Life in Society,* edited by Thomas E. Lasswell, J. Burma, and S. Aronson. Chicago: Scott Foresman & Co., 1965. Pp. 144–55.

TAWNEY, R. H. *Equality.* New York: Barnes & Noble, 1964.

THUROW, LESTER. *The Impact of Taxes on the American Economy.* New York: Praeger Publishers, 1971.

———, and LUCAS, ROBERT E. B. *The American Distribution of Income: A Structural Problem.* Washington, D.C.: Government Printing Office, 1972.

TITMUSS, RICHARD M. *Essays on the Welfare State.* New Haven, Conn.: Yale University Press, 1959.

———. *Income Distribution and Social Change.* London: Allen & Unwin, 1962.

———. Introduction to *Equality,* by R. H. Tawney. New York: Barnes & Noble, 1964.

TOBIN, JAMES. "Raising the Incomes of the Poor." In *Agenda for the Nation,* edited by Kermit Gordon. Washington, D.C. Brookings Institution, 1968. Pp. 77–116.

TUMIN, MELVIN M. "On Inequality." *American Sociological Review,* vol. 28 (February 1963), pp. 19–26.

———. "Some Principles of Stratification: A Critical Analysis." *American Sociological Review,* vol. 18 (August 1953), pp. 387–93.

UPTON, LETITIA, and LYONS, NANCY. *Basic Facts: Distribution of Personal Income and Wealth in the United States.* Cambridge, Mass.: Cambridge Institute, 1972.

WALLICH, HENRY C. "Inequality and Growth." In *Inequality and Poverty,* edited by Edward C. Budd. New York: W. W. Norton & Co., 1967. Pp. 14–26.

WATTS, HAROLD. "Income Redistribution: How It Is and How It Can Be." Unpublished paper for the Democratic Platform Hearings, St. Louis, June 17, 1972.

WEDDERBURN, DOROTHY, ed. *Poverty, Inequality and Class Structure.* Cambridge: Cambridge University Press, 1973.

YOUNG, MICHAEL. *The Rise of the Meritocracy.* Baltimore: Penguin Books, 1958.

YUCHTMAN, EPHRAIM. "Reward Distribution and Work Role Attractiveness in the Kibbutz." *American Sociological Review,* vol. 37 (October 1972), pp. 581–96.

ZABLOCKI, BENJAMIN. *The Joyful Community.* Baltimore: Penguin Books, 1971.

INDEX

About the Author

Born in Cologne, Germany, in 1927, Herbert J. Gans came to this country at the age of thirteen. He received his M.A. in social science from the University of Chicago and his Ph.D. in city planning from the University of Pennsylvania. By profession both a sociologist and a planner, he is well known for his writings on many aspects of the current American scene, including community life and city planning, urban renewal, the War on Poverty, popular culture, and the mass media. Currently Professor of Sociology at Columbia University and Senior Research Associate at the Center for Policy Research in New York City, he is the author of *The Urban Villagers, The Levittowners* (also available in Vintage Books), *People and Plans,* and a great many articles and professional journals.

V-623   KRADITOR, AILEEN S.   *Means and Ends in American Abolitionism*

V-367   LASCH, CHRISTOPHER   *The New Radicalism in America*

V-560   LASCH, CHRISTOPHER   *The Agony of the American Left*

V-488   LYND, STAUGHTON   *Intellectual Origins of American Radicalism*

V-502   MATTHEWS, DONALD R.   *U. S. Senators and Their World*

V-552   MAYER, ARNO J.   *Politics and Diplomacy of Peacemaking*

V-386   McPHERSON, JAMES   *The Negro's Civil War*

V-318   MERK, FREDERICK   *Manifest Destiny and Mission in American History*

V-84   PARKES, HENRY B.   *The American Experience*

V-371   ROSE, WILLIE LEE   *Rehearsal for Reconstruction*

V-212   ROSSITER, CLINTON   *Conservatism in America*

V-285   RUDOLPH, FREDERICK   *The American College and University: A History*

V-394   SEABURY, PAUL   *Power, Freedom and Diplomacy*

V-279   SILBERMAN, CHARLES E.   *Crisis in Black and White*

V-52   SMITH, HENRY NASH   *Virgin Land*

V-345   SMITH, PAGE   *The Historian and History*

V-432   SPARROW, JOHN   *After the Assassination: A Positive Appraisal of the Warren Report*

V-388   STAMPP, KENNETH M.   *The Era of Reconstruction 1865-1877*

V-253   STAMPP, KENNETH M.   *The Peculiar Institution*

V-110   TOCQUEVILLE, ALEXIS DE   *Democracy in America*, Vol. I

V-111   TOCQUEVILLE, ALEXIS DE   *Democracy in America*, Vol. II

V-103   TROLLOPE, MRS. FRANCES   *Domestic Manners of the Americans*

V-516   ULAM, ADAM B.   *The Unfinished Revolution*

V-540   VER STEEG, CLARENCE L. and RICHARD HOFSTADTER (eds.) *Great Issues in American History, 1584-1776*

V-265   WARREN, ROBERT PENN   *The Legacy of the Civil War*

V-605   WILLIAMS, JOHN A. and CHARLES F. HARRIS (eds.)   *Amistad 1*

V-660   WILLIAMS, JOHN A. and CHARLES F. HARRIS (eds.)   *Amistad 2*

V-362   WILLIAMS, T. HARRY   *Lincoln and His Generals*

V-208   WOODWARD, C. VANN   *Burden of Southern History*